Building Leaders

SpiritBuilt Leadership 4

Malcolm Webber

Published by:

Strategic Press
www.StrategicPress.org

Strategic Press is a division of Strategic Global Assistance, Inc.
www.sgai.org

2601 Benham Avenue
Elkhart, IN 46517
U.S.A.

+1-574-295-4357
Toll-free: 888-258-7447

ISBN 978-1-888810-65-3

All Scripture references are from the New International Version of the Bible, unless otherwise noted.

Printed in the United States of America

Table of Contents

Effective Leader Development Will Be Intentional

Introduction

In many countries, the church of Jesus Christ is growing at an extraordinary rate. This great blessing has brought with it great challenges. Possibly the greatest challenge of all is the current lack of quality leadership faced by many churches and church movements around the world.

The history of revivals informs us that the great harvest of one generation will be lost in the next if there are not sufficient leaders able to lead God's people to maturity.

God's people need leaders. Without leadership, the people are scattered (Matt. 26:31).

Just before he died, Moses looked at Israel and he cried out to God to provide leadership:

> Moses said to the LORD, "May the LORD, the God of the spirits of all mankind, appoint a man over this community to go out and come in before them, one who will lead them out and bring them in, so the LORD's people will not be like sheep without a shepherd." (Num. 27:15-17)

Similarly, Jesus looked at the multitudes and He told His disciples to pray that God would provide leaders:

> Jesus went through all the towns and villages, teaching in their synagogues, preaching the good news of the kingdom and healing every disease and sickness. When he saw the crowds, he had compassion on them, because they were harassed and helpless, like sheep without a shepherd. Then he said to his disciples, "The harvest

is plentiful but the workers are few. Ask the Lord of the harvest, therefore, to send out workers into his harvest field." (Matt. 9:35-38)

Building leaders was one of the main purposes of Jesus' ministry. At the earliest period of His ministry, Jesus began to gather around Him a company of disciples, in order to prepare them to carry on His work. From the start, Jesus wanted not only to have followers and disciples, but men whom He would train to lead and disciple others (Matt. 4:19). The training He would give these men was the principal part of His earthly ministry (John 17:6).

God's people need leaders. But not just any leaders will do – we need healthy leaders!

To be effective, churches and Christian organizations need healthy leaders who nurture the development of other healthy leaders at every level – this is a vital part of a healthy organizational culture.

To build more healthy leaders is a core responsibility of every existing leader in the church. The ultimate test of a leader is not whether he makes smart decisions and takes effective action in the short term, but whether he teaches others to be leaders and builds a community that can continue to be healthy and to thrive when he himself is not around.

The effective leader is not only a continuous *learner* himself; he must also be a continuous *teacher* and *builder* of others. He must pass along what he has learned to others who will in turn pass their learning along to others. As we will see, leaders build leaders!

Jesus built His disciples who then turned the world upside down. Look at Jesus' desire:

> *Most assuredly, I say to you, he who believes in Me, the works that I do he will do also; and greater works than these he will do, because I go to My Father. (John 14:12, NKJV)*

This is the desire of the truly great leader: to build other leaders who will entirely outdo him! His goal is to raise up leaders who will stand on his shoulders and who will then raise up more leaders who will stand on their shoulders and so forth.

The Bible is replete with examples of leaders who built leaders. Moses built Joshua, who took Israel into Canaan. David was a mighty warrior, and built other warriors. Elijah built Elisha, and the latter performed twice the number of miracles! Paul built leaders who built leaders; for example Paul built Aquila and Priscilla, who helped build Apollos. This was Paul's method:

> And the things you have heard me say in the presence of many witnesses entrust to reliable men who will also be qualified to teach others. (2 Tim. 2:2)

Effective leaders personally invest time and spiritual and emotional energy into building other leaders. Moreover, they expect all other leaders to do the same. Thus, the effective church or Christian organization is not just a "doing" organization, but it is a learning and teaching organization. Its way of life is continuous learning and teaching – at all levels. Building leaders is a central activity of the effective church or organization. It is hard-wired into everything everyone does. It is every leader's responsibility to nurture and expect leadership everywhere. This must become the mindset that pervades our churches and Christian organizations. Building a leader-building culture is the ultimate act of leadership. We need leaders who will build leaders.

Moreover, leadership is in all of us. With learning and practice we can all do better.

This is not to suggest that everyone is called to be an "organizational leader" such as a pastor or a business executive – someone with a formal, positional status of "leader." We all have very different callings (1 Cor. 12). However, there are several universal *kinds* of leadership:

- Personal leadership. We are all called to take responsibility for our own lives, moving ahead to fulfill God's purposes.
- Family leadership. The parents – in particular, the father – are the God-appointed leaders of the family.
- Relational leadership. At certain times, we are all called to take responsibility for helping others move ahead in their own lives.
- Spontaneous leadership. There will be times in almost everyone's life when sudden circumstances require that we lead others in certain ways.
- Organizational leadership. This is the formal role of leadership.

Thus, while we are not all called to be formal, "organizational leaders," there are many contexts in our lives in which we all are, nevertheless, "leaders."

Thus, "leader development" is *everyone's* responsibility!

Building healthy leaders is, however, easier said than done. It is not sufficient merely to send someone to a seminar or to give him a book on leadership to read. Leader development is highly complex and very little understood. Consequently, in many (perhaps most) churches and organizations, it is essentially left up to chance. We pay lip service to it, but devote little time to this endeavor. The small efforts at leader development that are made are often haphazard and not part of any overall cohesive strategy. Apart from sending young people to Bible school, usually we simply hope that the leaders will somehow raise themselves up! When asked what his leader development strategy was, one leader said, "You just have to let the cream rise to the top." In other words, "We have no intentional strategy for leader development; we're just hoping for the best!"

As a result, many times, efforts at leader development focus on courses and curriculum – the content. Not much time is spent on developing an appropriate *process* of development, which includes context as well as content.

Jesus' method of building leaders is summarized in Mark 3:

> *He appointed twelve – designating them apostles – that they might be with him and that he might send them out to preach and to have authority to drive out demons. (Mark 3:14-15)*

In this simple but profound statement, we have a distillation of how Jesus built leaders. In short, Jesus created a *transformational context* around His emerging leaders:

1. A *spiritual* environment, involving relationship with God (with Himself, as well as with the Father through prayer).
2. A *relational* web, involving relationship with a mature leader (Himself), and relationships with others (the community of the disciples).
3. An *experiential* context, involving challenging assignments, pressure and a diversity of learning opportunities.

Then, in that transformational context, He instructed them – the *content* of development.

In a nutshell, that was how Jesus built leaders. Thus, context + content = the process of leader development.

Usually, in leader development design we have focused on instruction. However, we must give significant attention to all four of the "dynamics of transformation." These are the 4Ds, the four dynamics of transformation:

- Spiritual – the transforming power of the Holy Spirit.
- Relational – the transforming power of relationships with others.
- Experiential – the transforming power of life's experiences.
- Instructional – the transforming power of the Word of God.

This was the practice of the early church:

They devoted themselves to the apostles' teaching and to the fellowship, to the breaking of bread and to prayer. (Acts 2:42)

They were "devoted" to all four dynamics of transformation:

- *the apostles' teaching* – instructional.
- *fellowship* – relational.
- *the breaking of bread* – experiential.
- *prayer* – spiritual.

This is how lives were changed in the New Testament church!

Through the spiritual dynamic, we come face-to-face with the inward Presence of the Holy Spirit, who transforms us:

And we all, with unveiled face, beholding the glory of the Lord, are being transformed into the same image from one degree of glory to another. For this comes from the Lord who is the Spirit. (2 Cor. 3:18, ESV)

Through the relational dynamic, we connect with people who reveal Christ to us and transform us:

From him the whole body, joined and held together by every supporting ligament, grows and builds itself up in love, as each part does its work. (Eph. 4:16; cf. Rom. 12:5; 1 Cor. 12:7; 1 Pet. 4:10)

The experiential dynamic includes the impact on us of many kinds of life's experiences. For example, in the sufferings, challenges and pressures of life, we go beyond our own capacities to succeed and, in a deeper way, look to God for His help, and we are changed:

… We were under great pressure, far beyond our ability to endure, so that we despaired even of life. Indeed, in our hearts we felt the sentence of death. But this happened that we might not rely on ourselves but on God, who raises the dead. (2 Cor. 1:8-9)

In the instructional dynamic, we are transformed by the Word of God, by the power of Truth:

> *... and how from infancy you have known the holy Scriptures, which are able to make you wise for salvation through faith in Christ Jesus. All Scripture is God-breathed and is useful for teaching, rebuking, correcting and training in righteousness, so that the man of God may be thoroughly equipped for every good work. (2 Tim. 3:15-17)*

When all 4Ds are strongly present in a design, spiritual life is nurtured, relational capacities are strengthened, character is developed, calling is clarified and deep leadership capacities are built.

> *Timothy, my son, I give you this instruction in keeping with the prophecies once made about you, so that by following them you may fight the good fight, (1 Tim. 1:18)*

All 4Ds are again present:

- *Timothy, my son,* – relational.
- *I give you this instruction* – instructional.
- *in keeping with the prophecies once made about you,* – spiritual.
- *so that by following them you may fight the good fight,* – experiential.

This was how Paul ministered the Gospel:

> *...our gospel came to you not simply with words, but also with power, with the Holy Spirit and with deep conviction. You know how we lived among you for your sake. You became imitators of us and of the Lord; in spite of severe suffering, you welcomed the message with the joy given by the Holy Spirit. And so you became a model to all the believers in Macedonia and Achaia. (1 Thess. 1:5-7)*

Once more, all 4Ds were present:

- *our gospel came to you not simply with words* – instructional.
- *but also with power, with the Holy Spirit and with deep conviction* – spiritual.
- *You know how we lived among you for your sake* – relational.
- *You became imitators of us and of the Lord* – experiential.
- *in spite of severe suffering* – experiential.

As a result, the lives of the Thessalonians were transformed and they became "a model to all the believers."

To build healthy leaders, *all* four dynamics of transformation must be strongly present; none can be neglected, all have the highest priority. This is the true challenge of Christian leader development – *to design and cultivate transformational cultures of leader development.*

Traditionally, we are more likely to seat our emerging leaders in neat rows behind desks and lecture them interminably in our attempts to build them. We are often very strong in our content but weak in the context we create for leader development. To be effective, the strength of the context must mirror the strength of the content.

The importance of context can be seen in the following story[1]:

> Bjorn is a Swedish immigrant to the U.S. He married a Swedish woman and they both live in Kalamazoo, Michigan. They have one son who is now six years old.
>
> Bjorn and his wife want their son to speak Swedish as well as English, so at home they try to speak Swedish to him as much as possible. They instruct him about the Swedish language, and encourage him, "You need to speak Swedish!"

---

[1] The names and personal details have been changed in this otherwise true story.

However, at school and in the local neighborhood, the only language spoken is, of course, English.

The little boy knows a few words of Swedish, but speaks English most of the time – even when he's at home, communicating to his parents who speak to him in Swedish. They are saddened by this and do not understand why he can't seem to learn Swedish very well.

In other words, *context often trumps content!* Consequently, we should give at least as much attention to designing context (the relational web and the spiritual and experiential environment) as we do to designing the instructional content.[2]

In another example, "Good seed can't make up for bad soil." The seed is like the content and the soil is like the context. A wise farmer will put a lot of energy into cultivating his soil. He knows that it takes more than good seed (curriculum) to raise a crop. So, a wise farmer intentionally cultivates the soil (the spiritual, relational, experiential context) before he plants the seed (starts teaching). So often, in our rush to get to the content we don't give much thought to cultivating the soil and we become like the man in Jesus' parable who just scatters seed. It should be no surprise that we so frequently have the three poor results mentioned in the parable.

We must change our approach to Christian leader development. For churches and Christian ministries to be effective in the 21st century, we must understand how leaders are built. Then we must develop intentional and holistic strategies.

---

[2] Although this distinction between context and content is a useful teaching tool to make a much-needed point, it is somewhat artificial. Our ultimate goal in leader development design is to seamlessly merge context and content into one united collage of transformation. In a good design, context and content will be relatively "seamless" – context becoming content, content becoming context; like many colors all coming together in one ray of light, like many threads becoming one garment.

To that end, in this book we will examine 18 principles of leader development, in six groups. Here are the six groups of principles.

Effective leader development will be:

- **Holistic.**
  Our goal must be to build the whole person.

- **Spiritual.**
  Our efforts at leader building must always be in submission to the work of the Holy Spirit.

- **Relational.**
  Leaders are built in a context of dynamic relationships with other people who are their mentors, role models, teachers, friends, and spiritual mothers and fathers.

- **Experiential.**
  Leader development is a hands-on experience. People learn by doing. Pressure is also essential in the formation of a leader.

- **Instructional.**
  The teaching of the Word of God must be practical, relevant and engaging.

- **Intentional.**
  We need an intentional design.

Within these six groups, here are the 18 principles, stated axiomatically:

	Effective leader development will be:
The Goal	**1. Holistic.** · The church needs healthy leaders.
The Process	**2. Spiritual.** · Ultimately, God is the One who builds leaders. · Prayer must saturate leader development.
	3. Relational. · Healthy leaders are built in community. · Leaders build leaders. · Leaders who build leaders should themselves be involved in the daily responsibilities of leadership. · Leaders are built a few at a time. · We must build the right ones!
	4. Experiential. · Leaders learn by doing. · Challenging assignments stretch and mature the emerging leader. · Leaders are built through fire.
	5. Instructional. · The Word of God is the foundation and the means for building healthy leaders. · Engagement brings change.
The Design	**6. Intentional.** · Responsibility for learning and growing is shared by the emerging leader and the church community. · Building leaders takes time. · People are different; so a variety of transformational experiences should be incorporated, and our goals should reflect their unique callings. · Both team and individual learning contexts must be provided. · Effective leader development is a complex, experiential collage.

Leader development will look different from nation to nation, from culture to culture, from situation to situation, from time to time; but these biblical principles will be effective anywhere.

Moreover, these principles can be applied in various situations:

- For those establishing new residential learning communities for emerging leaders.
- For those seeking to improve existing seminaries or Bible schools.
- For those who do short-term trainings for existing leaders.
- For those involved in teaching or mentoring emerging or existing leaders in *any* formal, non-formal or informal environment.
- For those wishing to establish a pervasive culture of "lifestyle people-building" in every ministry, family, business, and relationship (Eph. 4:16; cf. Eph. 6:4; Deut. 11:18-21; Tit. 2:3-5; Matt. 28:19-20).

This list of 18 principles is not complete; hopefully, it will inspire you to identify and collect additional attributes of effective leader development.

However, this list is, for now at least, a good place to start. These principles will work as you apply them in the wisdom the Holy Spirit gives you as you join Him in this great task of building leaders.

Malcolm Webber, Ph.D.
Elkhart, Indiana
January, 2003

Part 1

Effective Leader Development Will Be:

Holistic

全面塑造，平衡发展

Holistic building, balanced development

The Church Needs Healthy Leaders

Leader development has three components:

- The *goal* – a clear definition of the healthy Christian leader.
- The *process* – the particular dynamics we will use to achieve the goal.
- The *design* – the "curriculum" or planned design of the process.

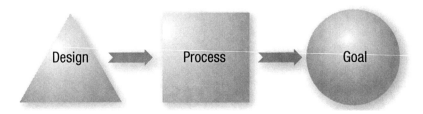

This is true for building anything. For example, before a builder starts building a house, he has a "vision" of what the completed house will look like – the goal.

Then, on the basis of the goal, he determines the kinds of things necessary to build the house – masonry, plumbing, carpentry, electrical work, finishing work, etc. – the process.

Then, he creates a detailed blueprint to guide the building process – the design.

No serious builder would simply begin throwing together bits of wood, nails, wires and plumbing and seeing what will happen (Luke 14:28-30).

Yet, that is so often what happens in Christian leader development – we piece together "good" courses and books and hope that something profitable will result.

To address the current crisis of leader development around the world, we need to step back from our traditional approaches and take a fresh look at our goal, process and design.

THE IMPORTANCE OF HAVING THE RIGHT GOAL

The very first step of designing an effective leader development strategy must be to clearly define the goal. Into what, exactly, are we trying to build the emerging leader? If our leader development efforts are successful, what will they produce? What will the leader "look like" at the end of an effective building process? And what will be the impact of his life and ministry?

Thus, we must first define the "ideal" Christian leader – or, in our language, the "healthy" Christian leader. This definition of the healthy Christian leader then becomes the goal of all leader development activities. The "process" – or all the various activities that we implement to build the leader – must directly correspond to the goal and help the emerging leader move toward the goal in his development.

This highlights the extreme importance of having the *right* goal. If the goal is not appropriate or adequate, then the process (which proceeds from the goal) will be insufficient and the leader development work itself will not be successful.

So, what is the "right" goal in Christian leader development?

Clearly, we do not merely need leaders; for the church to be led to maturity, we need *healthy* leaders. The church will not rise above the quality of its leaders.

> *A student is not above his teacher, nor a servant above his master.* (Matt. 10:24)

The healthy Christian leader will be strong in all five areas of Christ, Community, Character, Calling and Competencies. [3] Therefore, an effective process of leader development will integrate all five focuses. Unfortunately, most efforts at building leaders focus only on competencies.

Leader development must include spiritual as well as natural preparation. Consider the following:

GOD DOES NOT WANT YOUR TRAINING, HE WANTS YOU![4]

In the past fifteen years I have met scores of young people who have given their training to the Lord, yet reserved themselves for themselves! It is one of the most subtle snares in our training today. Musicians want to give their developed abilities to God. Mechanics, doctors, teachers, nurses, linguists, pilots and even preachers – all want to dedicate their training unto Him for His service. It just seems right and proper, so we have become accustomed to this procedure. Bible colleges and seminaries turn out graduates by the hundreds who are professionally trained for service. Yet amid all this, we have an inner hesitancy and a gnawing conviction: *something is wrong.*

There can be no doubt but that God is concerned with training. The question is this: *what kind of training?* We must discover the difference between natural and spiritual preparation.

We read that Moses "was learned in all the wisdom of the Egyptians." Philo credited Moses with proficiency in arithmetic, geometry, poetry, music, philosophy, astrology and various branches of education. Officially recognized as the son of Pharaoh's daughter, learned in all the wisdom of the Egyptians, with the best education of his day, Moses had every right to dream his dreams of a great

---

[3] Please see *Healthy Leaders: SpiritBuilt Leadership #2* by Malcolm Webber for a complete discussion of this model of healthy leadership.
[4] Quoted from *No Other Foundation* by DeVern Fromke.

career in Egypt, in the field of his training. He could serve both his people and his God.

We know then what a momentous choice it was for Moses, when he "was come to years," to renounce his favored position as son of the Palace, with all the social pleasures, the political privileges of his set, and "the treasures in Egypt." If we could have our way with him, we would rush him into a new sphere of service for God. Or better still, we would rush him off to Bible school for some specialized training in Christian work.

But here is the snare! There is many a "Moses" who has just come from Bible school and is wholly trained in the religious methods of our day. He has passed the courses on *how to do it*. How to promote a successful Sunday School. How to develop an adequate music program.

And having learned in homiletics how to preach, or in speech class how to hold the audience spell-bound, he is now ready to enter the ministry. But I wonder if this is not the very juncture where Moses stood? God would remind us that whatever our professional or formal training may be – He has a special course in spiritual preparation. Is Moses willing to enroll in the divine school of hard and humbling work, in solitude, adversity, danger, defeat, misunderstanding, slander and humiliation? It is not surprising that the man who emerged from the wilderness schoolroom was a man of great meekness, faith and faithfulness, spiritual boldness and intimacy with God.

Moses must have known he was called as Israel's deliverer. Did he ever wonder about wasting his training as he minded Jethro's sheep in Midian? George M. Cowan has suggested:

It was Moses the man, the product of all his training, that God used. Formal training seems to fade into the background as a matter of prime importance. Before God could use him, He had to break him – position, prestige, power, training: all had to go on the altar with life itself. Then God used him, including his training, in ways His own wisdom deemed best. Who else could have challenged the wise men of Egypt, explained and applied the God-given moral, social and practical laws to a people raised in Egypt, as did Moses? God used his training, but there is absolutely no hint that this was any part of God's argument in guiding Moses into a knowledge of, and willingness to do, His will. Moses had already turned his back on *all* before God used him and it.

This is God's way. He asks us to yield our training to Him, not to be used – but to go into death. Then out of that awful losing our natural abilities and (even) religious training, He brings us *into life.* Thus He puts all our training into a totally new perspective.

May the Spirit of revelation help us to see that God only wants *us.* Our training – religious and even spiritual – He takes into death that out of resurrection He might bring forth a totally new kind of Spirit-wrought development and thus a spiritual ministry and service unto God.

In leader development, we must start with the right goal – the building of the whole person. We must build all five elements of the healthy leader:

- Christ – the leader's spiritual life.
- Community – the leader's relational life.
- Character – the leader's integrity.
- Calling – the leader's vision.
- Competencies – the leader's knowledge and practical ministry skills.

It is not enough merely to build academic knowledge. We must build the whole person – that is the right goal of Christian leader development.

THE PROCESS MUST MATCH THE GOAL

Having defined our goal, we then must determine the right process to achieve that goal; and the process must match the goal. If our goal is entirely academic, then a purely academic process is appropriate. But if the goal of Christian leader development is the building of the whole person (healthy leaders) then the process also must be holistic – a purely academic process will not work.

This is a challenge currently faced by many Christian institutions. They have realized the need for the development of character, spiritual life and practical ministry competencies, but they have not yet realized the need for an entirely different process. They have found a new goal, but they are trying to reach that goal with an old process. Classroom lectures will not build character – even if those lectures are on the subject of character! The new wine demands a new wineskin. A holistic goal demands a holistic process. We must change the way we build leaders.

According to the ConneXions model, there are four necessary components in a holistic process. These are the four "dynamics of transformation":

- Spiritual – the transforming power of the Holy Spirit.
- Relational – the transforming power of relationships with others.
- Experiential – the transforming power of life's experiences.
- Instructional – the transforming power of the Word of God.

To transform people's lives, to build healthy leaders, we must incorporate all four dynamics in our leader development processes.

The following chapters will examine each of these four dynamics.

After having read or reviewed *Healthy Leaders: SpiritBuilt Leadership #2* by Malcolm Webber, individually or in your study group:

1. Please discuss how each of these five areas (Christ, Community, Character, Calling, Competencies) can intentionally be developed in the life of an emerging leader.

2. Please discuss how each of these five areas can be evaluated or observed in a leader's life.

3. Please find biblical examples of the presence of each of these five areas in the life of a leader.

4. Please evaluate your own life:
    a. What are your present strengths and weaknesses in each of these five areas?
    b. Identify the previous dealings of God in your life in each of these five areas? What has God done to build each of these areas in you?

Part 2

Effective Leader Development Will Be:

Spiritual

尊神为主，祷告开路

**God takes the lead,
while prayer opens up the way**

Ultimately, God Is the One Who Builds Leaders

GOD HIMSELF IS THE ULTIMATE AND PERFECT LEADER

God takes leadership very seriously. It is not a peripheral issue to Him. God Himself is the original, ultimate and perfect Leader of the entire universe – spiritual and physical.

> *...God, the blessed and only Ruler, the King of kings and Lord of lords, (I Tim. 6:15)*

God is Kings of all kings, Lord of all lords, and Leader of all leaders. He Himself is the Image of perfect leadership to which we aspire.

GOD CREATED LEADERSHIP

As the Leader of all things, God created a universe that needs leadership at every level. In the spiritual realm, angels have leaders. In the animal world, there are leaders. Likewise in the human world, people need leaders.

LEADERSHIP IS AN ETERNAL ACTIVITY

Moreover, God is building leaders not only for this life but also for eternity. You might have wondered about the efficiency of God taking an entire lifetime to prepare a mighty man or woman through all the trials and labors of life, only to have them depart from this world for the next, just when they are old and finally mature and wise enough to be of great use to everyone!

If God were only preparing them for leadership in this life, then such a thing would be inefficient and wasteful. However, God uses this life to build leaders for eternity.

Leadership is an eternal activity. A number of passages in both testaments demonstrate that many of the redeemed will reign (or lead) with Jesus in His Kingdom:

> *See, a king will reign in righteousness and rulers will rule with justice. (Is. 32:1)*

> *Jesus said to them, "I tell you the truth, at the renewal of all things, when the Son of Man sits on his glorious throne, you who have followed me will also sit on twelve thrones, judging the twelve tribes of Israel." (Matt. 19:28; cf. Luke 22:29-30)*

> *His master replied, "Well done, good and faithful servant! You have been faithful with a few things; I will put you in charge of many things. Come and share your master's happiness!" (Matt. 25:21)*

> *To him who overcomes, I will give the right to sit with me on my throne, just as I overcame and sat down with my Father on his throne. (Rev. 3:21)*

> *You have made them to be a kingdom and priests to serve our God, and they will reign on the earth. (Rev. 5:10; cf. Ps. 45:16; Is. 1:26; 24:23; 53:12; Jer. 3:15; 23:4; Dan. 7:22; 1 Cor. 6:2-3; Rev. 2:26-27)*

In Luke 19, Jesus shares a parable relating to His returning and the establishing of His kingdom on this earth:

> *He was made king, however, and returned home. Then he sent for the servants to whom he had given the money, in order to find out what they had gained with it. The first one came and said, "Sir, your mina has earned ten more." "Well done, my good servant!" his master replied. "Because you have been trustworthy in a very small matter,*

take charge of ten cities." The second came and said, "Sir, your mina has earned five more." His master answered, "You take charge of five cities." (Luke 19:15-19)

Revelation 20 also indicates that the redeemed will have various leadership responsibilities during the Millennium:

I saw thrones on which were seated those who had been given authority to judge. And I saw the souls of those who had been beheaded because of their testimony for Jesus and because of the word of God. They had not worshiped the beast or his image and had not received his mark on their foreheads or their hands. They came to life and reigned with Christ a thousand years.... Blessed and holy are those who have part in the first resurrection. The second death has no power over them, but they will be priests of God and of Christ and will reign with him for a thousand years. (Rev. 20:4-6)

Finally, Revelation 22 reveals that the saints will reign forever in God's eternal kingdom:

There will be no more night. They will not need the light of a lamp or the light of the sun, for the Lord God will give them light. And they will reign for ever and ever. (Rev. 22:5)

Thus, leadership itself is an eternal activity. Leadership is not something that is necessary in this life only because of the effects of sin, but from the beginning and for eternity, God intended men to exercise leadership.

Leadership is an eternal activity. Therefore, leader development in this life is part of our preparation for eternity. That's how important it is!

In many areas of life, one gets slower as one gets older. For example, an athlete slows down as he gets older. He is not as strong or as fast as he once was. But a leader can get better and better for his entire life!

Everyone who competes in the games goes into strict training. They do it to get a crown that will not last; but we do it to get a crown that will last forever. (1 Cor. 9:25)

Thus, like godliness, growth in leadership has "value for all things, holding promise for both the present life and the life to come" (cf. 1 Tim. 4:8).

GOD IS THE ONE WHO BUILDS LEADERS

Since God is building leaders for eternity, He takes personal responsibility for it now.

Ultimately, God is the One who raises up leaders. Leader development does not only happen when one completes a course on leadership or goes to "leadership school"; it happens all the time. Your course is neither the beginning nor the end of leader development in the lives of your emerging leaders. All the events of life – good and bad – contribute to one's growth as a leader. When we understand leader development in terms of life's processes, and not merely as the result of "education" or "training," we realize who the academic dean really is: God! God designs our lives and experiences uniquely and perfectly so that we can graduate with balance and maturity as leaders with whom He will be pleased to reign for eternity!

And we know that in all things God works for the good of those who love him, who have been called according to his purpose. (Rom. 8:28)

PRACTICAL IMPLICATIONS FOR BUILDERS

Since the Holy Spirit is the One who builds leaders, our processes of leader development must strive to allow Him to always have His way.

For we are God's fellow workers; you are God's field, you are God's building. (1 Cor. 3:9, NKJV).

Our agenda must never prevent God from accomplishing His. The builder must continually watch the Holy Spirit to see what He is doing and then cooperate with Him – rather than merely run through a pre-planned program of training or teaching. The builder must be flexible and must always be watching, sensitive to what God is doing. At a moment's notice, the agenda must shift to reflect God's will at that time for His emerging leader, taking advantage of serendipitous and Spirit-led events that will be profitable for the emerging leader's learning and growth.

Leader development is very important to God. He does not delegate this task entirely to us, but He remains actively and continually involved Himself. Our responsibility as builders is to see what He is doing and to cooperate with that.

Moreover, in our leader development processes we must help the emerging leader to understand the true intention of God in all his life's experiences. One's life is like a work of needlepoint. When viewed from underneath, it is a confused mass of thread with no pattern or meaning. However, from the top – from God's perspective – we can see the beauty of the intricate pattern; all the threads actually have meaning and purpose! With God, no experience is wasted, no event is so small as to be insignificant, no hardship so unpleasant as to be ignored. God uses it all, and the emerging leader must learn to understand how it all fits together.

The building process of God in the emerging leader's life didn't begin at the start of his involvement with a builder. Therefore, the role of the builder is to help the emerging leader properly understand the previous events of his life and relate them to the long-term purposes of God for his life. This can be done, for example, through reflection on the events, relationships and purposes of one's life.[5]

Furthermore, the building process of God in the emerging leader's life will not stop at the end of his involvement with a builder. Therefore, the role of a builder is to help the emerging leader properly prepare for the future events of his life so he can best respond to them.

---

[5] For more on this, please see Chapter 10 in *Purpose* by Malcolm Webber.

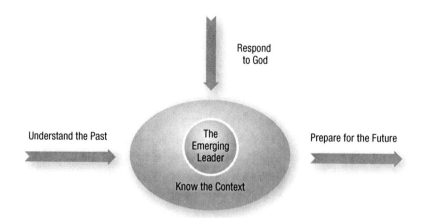

In summary, the threefold responsibility of the builder to the emerging leader is to help him:

- Understand the *past* working of God in his life and ministry.
- Recognize his immediate context of life and ministry and respond to God's *present* dealings.
- Prepare for the *future* working of God in his life and ministry.

Finally, we must recognize that a leader capable of leading God's people into the future is one of the scarcest resources in the church today. Consequently, a Christian organization that is successful in raising up new leaders will likely become a net "exporter" of its leaders to other churches and ministries. This is to be expected due to the general scarcity of effective Christian leaders. Knowing this in advance can help us to adopt the right attitude. God has called us to be givers and not hoarders. It is far better to "send" our leaders out as a gift to the Body of Christ and to the Kingdom purposes of God, than to think of them as having been "stolen" by another organization! Ultimately, we're all on the same team, serving the same Leader. He is the One building us, for His purposes.

Individually or in your study group:

1. Please find scriptures that demonstrate God's sovereignty over the building process.

    For example, when God allowed the young man David to confront the lion and bear, it was no accident (1 Sam. 17:34-37). Neither were the implications of this event limited to taking care of sheep. God was teaching David to trust in Him in order to be the future warrior king of Israel:

    > ...*The* LORD *that delivered me out of the paw of the lion, and out of the paw of the bear, he will deliver me out of the hand of this Philistine...* (1 Sam. 17:37)

2. Please reflect on your own life and identify specific ways in which God has sovereignly built you as a leader.

Prayer Must Saturate Leader Development

Our leader development process must revolve around prayer. Jesus and Paul consistently prayed *for* (Luke 22:32; cf. Col. 1:28 – 2:1; Gal. 4:19; 2 Tim. 1:3), *with* (Luke 11:1) and *over* their emerging leaders ((1 Tim. 4:14; cf. 2 Tim. 1:6).

Moreover, Jesus chose His new leaders in prayer. He was about to commit his entire future world-wide agenda to only a few men, so they had better be the right ones!

> *One of those days Jesus went out to a mountainside to pray, and spent the night praying to God. When morning came, he called his disciples to him and chose twelve of them, whom he also designated apostles... (Luke 6:12-13)*

Jesus chose the men His Father led Him to. He chose the men He saw in prayer.

> *...I tell you the truth, the Son can do nothing by himself; he can do only what he sees his Father doing, because whatever the Father does the Son also does. (John 5:19)*

Today, however, instead of praying about men and women, we spend our time thinking about strategies and techniques. Our focus is more on methods; Jesus' focus was on men. Our time is spent with each other in planning and strategizing; Jesus' time was spent with His Father in communion and fellowship. His inward union with His Father was the source of His success in building leaders.

If we are to excel in building leaders, our ministries must be born out of inward, living union with God.

...If a man remains in me and I in him, he will bear much fruit; apart from me you can do nothing. (John 15:5)

Jesus chose His leaders in prayer, and prayer was His first priority as He continued to build them. To succeed, we must do the same.

Furthermore, Jesus not only prayed Himself, but He taught His disciples how to pray by His words and works.

- They knew He spent entire nights in communion with His Father (Mark 1:35-37; Luke 6:12-13; Matt. 14:23).
- He not only prayed alone but also in the company of His disciples (Luke 11:1; 3:21; 9:28; Matt. 26:36). Jesus didn't merely teach a course on prayer; His disciples watched him pray. After one of these times, his disciples were so conscious of their own comparative incapacity for prayer, they requested, "Lord, teach *us* to pray" (Luke 11:1).
- In response to this request, Jesus taught them a simple form of prayer (Luke 11:2-4) and then shared one story emphasizing the need for perseverance in prayer (Luke 11:5-8) and another revealing the simplicity of faith in prayer (Luke 11:9-13).
- At other times, Jesus taught them on prayer (Matt. 6:5-13; 21:21-22; Mark 11:22-26; Luke 18:1-7; John 16:23-24).

Jesus knew God Himself and He led His disciples to know the Father also. John the Baptist also built his leaders the same way: he taught them to pray.

Prayer pervaded Paul's life and ministry (Gal. 4:19; Col. 1:29 – 2:3; etc.). He taught his disciples how to pray by his teaching and preeminently by his example.

Those who Jesus built as leaders went on to do it the same way with the leaders they built:

We proclaim to you what we have seen and heard, so that you also may have fellowship with us. And our fellowship is with the Father and with his Son, Jesus Christ. (1 John 1:3)

John, the apostle, says the entire purpose of his sharing the gospel was to bring people into the experience of fellowship with God.

This is one of the first responsibilities of a leader who is building another: *he must lead him to know God.*

Few people will find God in a deep way by themselves. This is true even of emerging leaders. Few leaders will learn to pray by themselves. They need to be taught.

Emerging leaders need to be taught not only how to pray, but how to live in continual inward union with God. As Jesus lived in continual fellowship with His Father, He revealed and modeled that life to the leaders He was building:

If you really knew me, you would know my Father as well. From now on, you do know him and have seen him…Anyone who has seen me has seen the Father… (John 14:7-9)

Both from Jesus' life and from His teaching, His new leaders learned to know the Father. They learned to pray. They learned to live in continual fellowship with God. They learned to trust God, to rely on Him in all situations. They learned to talk to God, to share with Him their deepest questions and struggles. They learned to look to God for everything – for the provision of all their needs, for the answers to all their questions. They learned to live in His presence. They learned to know God. Jesus taught them this.

In saying this, we again draw a vast contrast with our modern methods of building leaders. Little, if any, attention is usually given to this great endeavor. Little time is devoted to teaching our new leaders to pray. Certainly we are busy teaching them *about* prayer, but do we teach them *to pray?* There is no lack of courses and books about prayer today, but we must give our new leaders more: we must teach them actually to pray, we must teach them actually to know God, not only to know some facts about Him.

Jesus revealed the Father to His disciples; they saw God, heard His voice and touched Him! The primary characteristic of an effective Christian leader is that he knows God and that he lives and ministers out of his inward union with God.[6] And our primary responsibility in building new leaders is to see that they know God – we must teach them to pray.

---

[6] Please see *Healthy Leaders: SpiritBuilt Leadership #2* by Malcolm Webber for more on this.

Individually or in your study group:

1. Please find biblical examples of the centrality of prayer in the life of a leader.

2. Please find biblical examples of leaders who led their disciples to grow in their personal relationships with God.

Part 3

Effective Leader Development Will Be:

Relational

真诚关系，群策群力

**Genuine relationship,
plus collective wisdom and efforts**

Healthy Leaders Are Built in Community

An ancient African proverb says, "It takes a village to raise a child." Similarly, it takes a spiritual community or family to build a leader.

God sovereignly raises up His leaders, but we also have a responsibility in the matter. We have to work at it. It does not happen automatically. Leader development is the responsibility of the entire local church. Churches must consciously, actively and deliberately build the present and next generations of leaders. In most churches, leader development is left entirely up to chance. What differentiates a church that raises up leaders from one that does not is a clear priority for, and some means of ensuring, developmental opportunities for its people. Churches that are serious about the present and future intentionally build leaders!

Moreover, this responsibility is not simply delegated to the "Leader Development Department." It is a community responsibility.

A COMPARISON OF THREE APPROACHES

In the traditional approach to building leaders, the local church sends its emerging leaders to a specialized, independent, external entity (Bible school, seminary, non-formal training program, etc.) – the "central factory" – that takes responsibility for training them and then sending them back[7]:

---

[7] If they ever make it back; many do not.

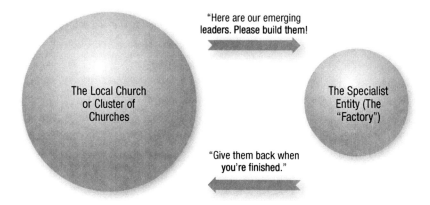

"Here are our emerging leaders. Please build them!

The Local Church or Cluster of Churches

The Specialist Entity (The "Factory")

"Give them back when you're finished."

This "factory" approach has greatly hindered the work of Christian leader development in several ways[8]:

- By limiting the numbers of leaders who can be trained to however many the relatively few specialist entities are able to cope with.
- By removing the students from the contexts of life and ministry that are vital to their development as people and as leaders.
- By siphoning off key leaders who, after their training in a city seminary, for example, do not return home since they prefer the new lifestyle or the greater opportunities now available to them. Many will try to find pastoral jobs in the city; if they're not able to do that, they simply obtain "regular" jobs there. This "brain drain" is a problem facing churches in many developing countries. The American consulate in Madras reported that in the late 1970s the "brain drain" among Indian theological students was 90 percent. This is one reason why hundreds of churches in India do not have pastors.
- By discouraging and disabling the local church communities

---

[8] This is not a wholesale criticism or rejection of theological education. Some Bible schools, seminaries and non-formal training programs are very good, some are very poor, and there are many in-between. The ones that are disconnected from the life and ministry of the local church and who are entirely academic in their focus are addressed here.

from assuming their vital responsibility for building their own emerging leaders. Sadly, this disconnect continues long after graduation, with the leader forever looking to outside influences for his growth and development.

- By introducing woefully inadequate declarations of qualification, confusing diplomas with actual capability.

- By introducing a spiritual "caste" system into the church: the degreed professionals are distinguished from the "lay people" who, in many cases, are actually more qualified to do the real work of the ministry.

- By wasting significant resources – financial resources spent in maintaining institutions, and years of people's lives spent studying many things that have no relation to useful ministry skills or inner spiritual capacities.

Thus, the "central factory" approach has undermined both the quantity and the quality of our Christian leaders, while damaging the spiritual and social dynamics of our churches.

We would never dream of sending our natural children off to another (more "expert") family to be brought up and then sent back to us when they're adults! Even though we recognize that some families are, in fact, better than others in raising children, we would not consider that the advantages of this "expertise" might outweigh the irreplaceable benefits of a child being raised by his own parents in his own family.

Strangely, however, when it comes to our spiritual sons and daughters, this is exactly what we do – we send them off to the "experts." We think we're supposed to do this! We must change our thinking: just as the natural family takes responsibility for bringing up its own children, so the church needs to reclaim this God-given responsibility of building our own leaders.

One of the main reasons why local churches see themselves as fundamentally incapable of building leaders is because they have been trained to view leader development as necessarily involving institutions, buildings, tenured professors with big degrees and salaries to match, accreditation, desks and dormitories, libraries containing thousands of books, etc. However, if our goal in leader development changes from scholarship to the development of the whole person, then suddenly we recognize that not only is the local church capable of building its own leaders, it is in fact, *the only place where it can properly occur!*

This is how church leaders were built in Acts – there is not a single instance of a seminary or Bible school that functions remotely from and independently of the local church. Biblically, the local church or cluster of churches is the primary unit of leader development.

The church has lost her ability to build and care for her leaders. This is a core reason for today's leadership crisis around the world. The following are recent statistics[9] concerning pastors in the U.S.:

- 50% feel unable to meet the needs of the job.
- 90% feel they are inadequately trained to cope with ministry demands.
- 46% say they have experienced depression or burnout to the extent that they needed to take a leave of absence from ministry.

Why do we keep doing our training the same way, when we know it is not working well?

A second approach is when the church has its own internal "Bible school" – in effect, a "local factory" – that takes responsibility for training new leaders. This is becoming a very popular approach today with the spread of church-based theological training; in essence, the seminary is brought to the church.

This has many advantages over the "central factory" approach, since the "local factory" will probably be more in touch with the church's own

---

[9] H.B. London Jr. and Neil B. Wiseman, *Pastors at Greater Risk* (Ventura, CA: Regal Books, 2003).

doctrines, beliefs, values and vision. Moreover, the participant will be able to maintain his existing relationships while he goes through his learning, and he will be considerably more likely to continue his life and ministry as a part of the church when he completes his learning.

However, this approach still has significant downfalls:

- The local church itself is still not vitally and personally involved in the building process. By itself, this represents a critical and fatal shortfall of the approach.
- Usually this approach represents an attempt simply to "relocate the seminary" to the local church. Much of the actual content of the training remains academic and theoretical. Moreover, since the local church lacks the resources of the seminary, the quality of this content is frequently diminished.
- This places too great a burden on the local leaders so that they are forced to compromise either the quality of their training work or the quality of their usual ministry responsibilities since they don't have the time and energy to do both well. A healthy building process needs to involve the whole church community, not only the "professionals"; moreover, it must be integrated into the life and ministry of the church and not become merely "one more thing" the leaders now have to do.
- It obscures and distracts us from the fact that much leader development – perhaps the most critical – does not occur

formally but casually in the context of the relationships and ministry responsibilities and opportunities of the local church.[10]

- This approach often maintains the educational "caste" structure of the traditional system, in which advancement within the church is tied not to proven spirituality or ministry capacity but to an academic degree obtained by writing papers and passing exams.

A third, and much healthier, approach is when leader development takes place in a "learning community" that is connected immersively and pervasively to the church community. In this model there should be considerable "cross-linking" between the church community and the learning community and no "walls" between them. *Leader development is integrated into the life and ministry of the local church or cluster of churches.* Thus, the biblical model is not only "church-based," it is "church-integrated."

---

[10] In many nations, where do the young people learn to play soccer? The homes, local parks and streets form the organic and spontaneous environment for skill development, mentoring and practice. Why can't the church adopt a similar model? Ted Ward once asked the author, "What was the hardest thing you ever learned to do?" After some thought I replied, "To speak." "That's right," he said. "The hardest thing people ever learn to do is to communicate in their first language, and they do it without going through a single course or class!"

The learning community cannot do it properly by itself. It takes a family to build a leader – a large family. Leaders are not formed in isolation but in community. If they are to be healthy, they need the nurture and support as well as the genuine accountability of the community. They need the spiritual mothers and fathers, the role models, the friends and the organic ministry opportunities that only the local church community can provide.

> *Their leader will be one of their own; their ruler will arise from among them... (Jer. 30:21)*

We must move from the "factory" approach back to the "family."

THE ROLE OF COMMUNITY IN THE LIFE OF A CHRISTIAN LEADER

Community serves a twofold place in the life of the Christian leader:

1. The healthy leader is *built* in community. No healthy leader will ever be built in a vacuum. Even the hottest embers grow cold in isolation.

   It is relatively easy to live victoriously when we are all by ourselves. The "spiritual lone ranger" is not tested as deeply as the man who lives in community. It is easy to be patient when no one is irritating us! It is when we come together that we have the opportunity to be patient, kind, forgiving and loving; to walk in servanthood and grace toward one another. As someone said, the Christian life would be easy if it weren't for the devil and people! In reality, we only really mature and grow as Christians in the context of community.

   > *As iron sharpens iron, so one man sharpens another. (Prov. 27:17)*

Do not lie to each other, since you have taken off your old self with its practices and have put on the new self, which is being renewed in knowledge in the image of its Creator. Here there is no Greek or Jew, circumcised or uncircumcised, barbarian, Scythian, slave or free, but Christ is all, and is in all. Therefore, as God's chosen people, holy and dearly loved, clothe yourselves with compassion, kindness, humility, gentleness and patience. Bear with each other and forgive whatever grievances you may have against one another. Forgive as the Lord forgave you. And over all these virtues put on love, which binds them all together in perfect unity. (Col. 3:9-14)

The leader is built in community. Jesus grew in community, subject to His parents and a part of the community around Him (Luke 2:41-52). Paul was built in community in the school of Gamaliel (Acts 22:3) and then in the church after he was saved (Acts 9:19, 27). According to church tradition, even the somewhat individualistic John the Baptist matured in community.

2. The leader *leads* in the context of community (Rom. 12:4-8; 1 Cor. 12:12-27).

    ...in Christ we who are many form one body, and each member belongs to all the others. (Rom. 12:5)

He never grows to the point where he no longer needs vital relationships with others around him. Effective Christian leaders lead in a context of community – not as tough "ministry islands" off by themselves. In the body of Christ, no members are independent (1 Cor. 12).

    The body is a unit, though it is made up of many parts; and though all its parts are many, they form one body. So it is with Christ. (1 Cor. 12:12)

49

Jesus had friends and He needed them. Jesus needed their fellowship and support.

> ...*My soul is overwhelmed with sorrow to the point of death. Stay here and keep watch with me. (Matt. 26:38)*

He was grieved when they fell asleep in the garden (Matt. 26:36-45).

Paul also had friends, and they nurtured and strengthened him:

> *You know that the household of Stephanas were the first converts in Achaia, and they have devoted themselves to the service of the saints. I urge you, brothers, to submit to such as these and to everyone who joins in the work, and labors at it. I was glad when Stephanas, Fortunatus and Achaicus arrived, because they have supplied what was lacking from you. For they refreshed my spirit and yours also... (1 Cor. 16:15-18)*

Significantly, Stephanas was Paul's own convert! Paul was not too proud to receive nurture and support from his own spiritual son. Onesiphorus also was a friend to Paul and strengthened him in "many ways," doubtless including emotionally and spiritually:

> *May the Lord show mercy to the household of Onesiphorus, because he often refreshed me and was not ashamed of my chains. On the contrary, when he was in Rome, he searched hard for me until he found me. May the Lord grant that he will find mercy from the Lord on that day! You know very well in how many ways he helped me in Ephesus. (2 Tim. 1:16-18)*

Romans 16:1-16 mentions several of Paul's "dear" friends and even a spiritual "mother" in verse 13!

Greet Rufus, chosen in the Lord, and his mother, who has been a mother to me, too. (Rom. 16:13)

If Jesus, the Son of God, and Paul, the mighty apostle, needed friends, who are we that we do not? It is not a sign of strength to be by yourself in leadership. It is a mark of weakness. Leaders need friends!

Thus, community serves a twofold place in the life of the leader:

1. The healthy leader is built in community.
2. The healthy leader leads in community

This does not refer merely to an ideological commitment to "community" but to genuine, committed, nurturing and accountable relationships. As Dietrich Bonhoeffer wrote, "He who loves community destroys community. He who loves the brothers builds community." The author has known people who loudly declared their great love for "New Testament church life"; it was people they were not too fond of!

Biblically, spiritual maturity is a corporate experience:

In him the whole building is joined together and rises to become a holy temple in the Lord. And in him you too are being built together to become a dwelling in which God lives by his Spirit.(Eph. 2:21-22)

so that Christ may dwell in your hearts through faith. And I pray that you, being rooted and established in love, may have power, together with all the saints, to grasp how wide and long and high and deep is the love of Christ, and to know this love that surpasses knowledge – that you may be filled to the measure of all the fullness of God. (Eph. 3:17-19)

…so that the body of Christ may be built up until we all reach unity in the faith and in the knowledge of the Son of God and become

mature, attaining to the whole measure of the fullness of Christ. (Eph. 4:12-13)

From him the whole body, joined and held together by every supporting ligament, grows and builds itself up in love, as each part does its work. (Eph. 4:16)

Healthy leadership does not exist as its own separate entity apart from or above the entire community.[11] Neither should leader development exist as a separate entity apart from the entire church community.

THE ENTIRE COMMUNITY MUST TAKE RESPONSIBILITY FOR LEADER DEVELOPMENT

In most Western organizations today, we love specialization and compartmentalization. Consequently, as we have already mentioned, it is common for us to entirely delegate the task of leader development to some "specialist" person or group – whether inside or outside the church. We identify the emerging leader who needs to be built and then send him to the "experts" to "do it" for us.

However, if it is to be done right, the existing leaders themselves must participate in the teaching and building of emerging leaders. They should not merely delegate this role to others. Leaders must personally act as coaches, role models, teachers and mentors. They must share their lives with those around them – their mistakes as well as their victories. True leaders are builders of leaders. Of course, as part of their general strategy of development, they may send the emerging leaders to a profitable training seminar or give them a good book to read, or receive advice or help from a consultant, etc., but they will not pass off the overall *responsibility* to anyone else. Leaders are best built by leaders in the context of normal life and ministry.

---

[11] Please see *Healthy Leaders: SpiritBuilt Leadership #2* by Malcolm Webber, for more on the role of the community in the life of a leader.

The ministry of an in-house learning community can be powerful, but it must be coupled with a broad responsibility across the church family to raise leaders.

Communities build leaders. It is not only the individual teaching or mentoring leader who is responsible for building the emerging leader. The entire church contributes to the growth of every new leader. In a variety of ways, a healthy church community works together (albeit not always consciously nor necessarily well) to give the emerging leader the experiences, challenges, learning opportunities, exposure to multiple leaders, role models, relationships, accountability, feedback, support, encouragement, prayer support, exchange of life, etc. that he or she needs.

> *I myself am convinced, my brothers, that you yourselves are full of goodness, complete in knowledge and competent to instruct one another. (Rom. 15:14)*

> *...When you come together, everyone has a hymn, or a word of instruction, a revelation, a tongue or an interpretation. All of these must be done for the strengthening of the church. (1 Cor. 14:26)*

> *Let the word of Christ dwell in you richly as you teach and admonish one another with all wisdom, and as you sing psalms, hymns and spiritual songs with gratitude in your hearts to God. (Col. 3:16)*

> *And we urge you, brothers, warn those who are idle, encourage the timid, help the weak, be patient with everyone. (1 Thess. 5:14)*

The builder must take steps to establish and maintain the appropriate overall environment for optimal development. Building leaders means working with the entire community, not just with the new leaders themselves – during the formal building process and also after the formal process. The process of building leaders is never finished.

The learning community should not attempt to replace the spiritual community in the building process, but the two must work integrally.

The role of the spiritual community in building leaders is twofold:

- During any formal process, the community must take responsibility for and must participate in the process.
- After any formal process, the community must take responsibility for the ongoing (and never-ending) building of the emerging or existing leader.

THE HEALTHY CHURCH

In the New Testament, the church is compared to the human body (e.g., 1 Cor. 12). When a part of someone's body is not functioning properly, that person is, by definition, sick or unhealthy. Thus, a simple definition of a "healthy" human body is one in which every member is functioning properly. In the same way, a healthy church is, quite simply, *one in which every member is functioning properly.*

There are many popular, and valuable, models of what constitutes a "healthy church." For example, a healthy church will have inspiring worship, need-oriented evangelism, loving relationships, etc. *If every member functions properly then the local church will have all these components.*

But, what does it mean to "function properly"? In Ephesians, Paul shares a clear revelation of this:

> *From Him the whole body, joined and held together by every supporting ligament, grows and builds itself up in love, as each part does its work. (Eph. 4:16)*

There are three things that each member must do in order for him or her to be considered "functioning properly."

First, each member must "grow." Personally and directly connected to the life of the Head ("from Him the whole body...") each member of the church must grow in spiritual maturity. In the church around the world, we're not doing too badly in this regard. Many Christians do take personal responsibility for their own spiritual lives. They know that God has called them to grow, and not to remain spiritual babies.

Second, each member must serve, or "do its work." Every member of the church is a "minister"; we all have a calling from God and the corresponding gifting. For the last couple of decades, there has been much teaching on "finding your gifting," etc., and the church has improved considerably in this regard. Many believers now have a clear vision for their own personal involvement in the ministry of their local churches. Of course, "serving" does not only involve "official ministry activity" but, even more importantly, also serving one another in the broad, practical context of daily life and relationships.

Third, each member must "build" others: "the body builds itself up." This has been the critical missing element in many churches. We have not taken deliberate, personal responsibility for building others. Usually we "delegate" that responsibility to others. So, for example, the children are taught spiritually at Sunday School, the new believers go to discipleship class on Tuesday night, the emerging leaders are sent off to Bible school, etc.

However, biblically, we *all* have responsibility to build others. Parents are responsible to build their children (Eph. 6:4; Deut. 6:4-9; 11:18-21). Existing believers are responsible to build the new disciples (Matt. 28:19-20). The older women are responsible to build the younger ones (Tit. 2:3-5). The mature men teach the younger men (2 Tim. 2:2).

A healthy church is one in which every member grows, serves and builds others. We must have all three. And all three must come from life – the indwelling life of Christ in each believer's life (John 15:4-5; Eph. 4:16) as he or she grows, serves and builds.

This is a profound paradigm shift for many believers and churches. It is a shift away from a program mentality to a people mentality. However, if we can create a church culture in which every believer takes responsibility to grow, serve and build, our churches will transform their worlds!

CHURCH-INTEGRATED LEADER DEVELOPMENT

If a healthy church, like a healthy body, is one in which every member is functioning properly, with every member growing, serving and building others, then the primary task of leader development is not so much to implement curriculum as it is to *create culture.*

"Culture" refers to shared beliefs, values, attitudes and actions. In a healthy church there is a *culture of leader development.* The primary task of leader development work is to create this culture and then to oversee it, nurture it and protect it.

If we can nurture and sustain cultures of "people-building" in our local churches, then we will be able to effectively address the current leader development crisis.

In Acts, the local churches, or clusters of churches, were the primary units of leader development. Typically, the churches did not send their emerging leaders off to be built somewhere else by someone else. Just as parents are, quite naturally, the best ones to build their own children, so churches in the New Testament themselves embraced the responsibility and privilege of building their own spiritual sons and daughters. Timothy, for example, was built in the life of the local churches at Lystra and Iconium before Paul took him along as part of his apostolic team (Acts 16:1-2; 1 Tim. 4:14; 2 Tim. 1:5; 3:14-15).

The local church is the most natural and most potent place to build the whole person. In the local church there is an extraordinary transformational environment of spiritual, relational, experiential and instructional dynamics. In the normal life and ministry of the local church there can be leaders building leaders, spiritual mothers and fathers, role models, examples, mentors, coaches, responsibilities, challenges, prayer and worship, the Presence of God, sufferings, instruction in the Truth of God's Word. All of this is already present in the local church – at least potentially.

Thus, as previously stated, the primary task of leader development is not so much to write and implement academic curriculum on biblical topics as it is to create and sustain culture – a culture within the local church of purposefully and wisely interacting with the spiritual, relational, experiential and instructional dynamics of the organic life of the church. Before the church was established, Jesus built leaders this way – in His learning community of disciples. Paul did this in his team. The local churches in Acts took responsibility for building their own sons and daughters in an experiential collage of diverse people, relationships, influences, assignments, tasks, responsibilities, duties, opportunities, pressures, crises, blessings, sufferings, rejections, successes, mistakes, etc., that all worked together to build the emerging leaders.

But, how do we get there?

Today, the idea of "church-sponsored theological instruction" is becoming increasingly popular.[12] While this represents a major improvement over the traditional practices of disconnected biblical teaching in remote academic institutions, yet it is still not the New Testament paradigm. The New Testament pattern is more along the lines of "church-integrated leader development." Here are two key contrasts:

First, true leader development is not merely a class lecture or a small group session that is "sponsored by the church" and that occurs in a room in the church building on Tuesday nights or all-day Saturday. Leader development needs to be *integrated* into the life of the church – truly owned by the church, occurring across the life of the church, all week long.

This is a difference of *process*. If our purpose was merely to get the right information into the heads of our emerging leaders, then lectures followed by papers and small group sessions to discuss the information

---

[12] The following general comments are not directed at any *specific* program, whether formal or non-formal.

(with degrees at the end to prove the information was mastered) would be sufficient. But if our goal is the building of the whole person, then a much more complex process is necessary – we need a transformational collage of spiritual, relational and experiential *as well as* instructional dynamics.

An effective leader development process is not a neat series of courses but a fiery immersion in real-life, real-time experiences, reflecting the complicated and fundamentally difficult nature of Christian leadership, bringing deep heart issues to the surface to be dealt with, and compelling the emerging leader to look utterly to God for everything in his life and ministry.

We need a culture of leader development – shared beliefs, values, attitudes and actions – across the life of the church, all week long. This is the healthy church: parents building their children (Eph. 6:4; Deut. 6:4-9; 11:18-21), existing believers building the new disciples (Matt. 28:19-20), older women building the younger ones (Tit. 2:3-5), mature men teaching the younger men (2 Tim. 2:2), people building people, leaders building leaders. Thus, church-sponsored is not enough; leader development must be truly church-integrated.

Second, "theological education" of the mind is entirely insufficient. The whole person must be built, with broad and deliberate attention given to the nurturing of spiritual life, relational capacity (including marriage, family, and relationships with others), character, vision and calling, as well as practical ministry capacities. The leader himself or herself must be built.

This is a difference of *goal*. The goal of New Testament leader development is not merely intellectual mastery of some biblical ideas, but rather transformation of life – the holistic building of the leader.

These are some of the many powerful advantages of this biblical paradigm:

First, in our experience, when local churches rediscover the organic New Testament pattern of church-integrated leader development, it affects the church as much as it affects the emerging leaders. Here is a recent testimony from an Asian church network leader:

> When we followed Jesus' leader development principles, the result has been a great flourishing of vigor and life in the church. All the members are functioning, building each other and growing together, thus bringing great growth and revival to the whole church.

Second, while church-sponsored theological instruction is usually accomplished in a limited time of training, church-integrated leader development is an ongoing, lifelong commitment to growing, serving and building together.

Third, church-sponsored theological instruction usually revolves around the set curriculum ("one size fits all"), whereas church-integrated leader development can effectively respond to the individual needs and callings of the emerging leaders.

We recognize that church-sponsored theological instruction is a sincere and significant improvement over traditional leader development approaches; however, the New Testament model is not so much church-sponsored theological instruction but rather church-integrated leader development.

If we can shift away from our Greek-rooted fixation on academic curriculum[13] and instead learn how to create and sustain organic cultures of healthy people-building within the life of our local churches, then, by God's grace, we will be able to effectively address the current leader development crisis.

---

[13] For more on this, please see *A Christian Critique of the University* by Charles Habib Malik, and *The Rise of Christianity* by W.H.C. Frend (Chapter 11 is especially illuminating: "The Third Century: Christian Platonism of Alexandria and Its Opponents, 190-275")

PRACTICAL IMPLICATIONS FOR BUILDERS

Our leader development efforts must not be conducted apart from a living community of people in which the emerging leaders function and participate.

First, those emerging leaders who are being trained must be formed into a community themselves, and not be allowed to exist as separate individuals. In our traditional systems of education, the individual students arrive at the class, sit at their separate desks, listen to the lectures, participate in whatever group tasks are required of them, then leave and go their own separate ways until the next class time. Whatever relationships and community they do form during their schooling are usually incidental and are rarely integrated into the schooling itself.

The best "leadership school" is *a transformational, learning community* in which all the participants take responsibility for each other, hold each other accountable, care for each other, pray together, worship and seek God together, work and serve together, struggle together, resolve conflicts, and learn and grow together.

It is significant that nowhere in the gospels do we find Jesus alone with one of His disciples. Even the interactions that appear to have taken place between Jesus and one person were always conducted with others close by. Certainly there are clear biblical examples of "one-on-one" mentoring such as Moses and Joshua or Elijah and Elisha, but it appears that Jesus always engaged in character building when the "family" was together.

In addition, some of the unhealthy dependencies and transferences of dysfunctionalities that we often see in mentoring relationships would be avoided by a community approach to building disciples and leaders.[14]

Second, as already stated, the community of emerging leaders must itself be part of a larger spiritual community. The learning community may be distinct but it must not be separate from the overall community. The two communities should not compete but should have one unified and integrated corporate strategy of leader development. This larger community might be a local church or cluster of churches.

Both the learning community and the larger community must take initiative in building the relationship between them. It will help in this regard if there is some overlap of direct leadership between the two communities. It will be particularly effective if the top leader of both is the same person; this will help greatly to create a strong level of ownership of the learning community by the larger, spiritual community.

The larger community can take responsibility for providing:

- Overall leadership of the learning community.
- Providing and sharing the vision.
- Practical provision – shelter, food, clothing. Significantly, this means the learning community does not need to be dependent upon outsiders for funding.[15] This, in turn, means that church-integrated learning communities can be multiplied almost limitlessly!

---

[14] In one-on-one mentoring, the various personal issues, prejudices and personality quirks of the mentor are sometimes reproduced in the mentee; there is a "transference of dysfunctionality," with *both* the good and bad things being passed on. However, if there are others involved in building the new leader (other leaders, spiritual mothers and fathers, mentors, coaches, intercessors, etc.), then the emerging leader is less likely to pick up the wrong things from one leader. This is a big advantage of the community approach as contrasted with a traditional mentoring, one-on-one approach where only one leader interacts with each emerging leader.
[15] Some outside financial support might be beneficial for initial start-up expenses in certain situations. Please see Chapter 6 of *Church Planting* by Malcolm Webber for more on the need for indigenous ministries to be self-supporting and how that relates to their own abilities to also be self-governing and self-propagating.

- Spiritual care and nurture – pastoring and shepherding. This spiritual care can occur in both formal and informal ways. Some possible formal roles might be:
  - Pastoral Coaches, who provide accountability, nurture and encouragement as the participant responds to the work of God in his or her heart (Christ, Community, Character).
  - Intercessors, who pray regularly for the participant (all 5Cs of Christ, Community, Character, Calling and Competencies).
  - Ministry Mentors, who provide ministry examples, practical and experiential guidance, advice, correction and encouragement as the student grows in understanding of his or her calling and in the competencies necessary to fulfill that calling (Calling, Competencies).
  - Learning Coaches: former participants in their own training who provide encouragement as well as practical help regarding the process.
  - Spiritual Friends: peers who can give encouragement, accountability and prayer support.
  - Host Families, who provide homes, clothing, food and relationship.
  - The spiritual community – spiritual mothers and fathers, brothers and sisters, friends, role models, mentors, ministry opportunities.
- Teaching and mentoring (both character and ministry).
- Modeling the various gifts and ministries.
- Sharing life stories.
- Life examples.
- Returning missionaries and traveling ministries sharing their stories.
- Encouragement.
- Oversight.
- Accountability.
- Prayer support.
- Learning materials and resources.
- Ministry opportunities and responsibilities.
- Housing for participants and their families.

- Ministry assignments after the formal learning period is over.
- Ongoing mentoring after the formal learning period is over.

The learning community can take responsibility for:

- Praying for the church.
- Being accountable to the church.
- Being committed to the church and sharing its burdens.
- Submitting to the church's vision.
- Providing various forms of ministry and service in the church community.
- Being examples and mentors to younger members of the church.
- Visiting the people to build relationships with them and looking for ways to serve – both spiritually and practically.
- Leading special combined meetings on a regular basis.
- Sharing the participants' visions with the church so there is mutual understanding.
- Providing reports on the participants' growth.
- Inviting counsel and advice.

By making the learning community an integral part of a larger spiritual community, the participants will experience a more holistic learning and growing experience.

We will also avoid the frequent problems associated with "re-entry" into normal life after the learning experience. For example, after going through an intense learning experience that has lasted for several months or years, participants will frequently experience difficulties in reconnecting with their local spiritual communities. It is not uncommon for them to go into depression, discouragement, confusion, isolation or other forms of emotional and intellectual disequilibrium after the artificial "high" of the learning time is over. This can partly be avoided when they *maintain* their relationships and responsibilities within their normal community throughout the learning experience.

In addition, the gap between knowledge and practical ministry that usually occurs in traditional schools will also be avoided. When the emerging leader is placed in a far-away school for training and nurtured in an artificial environment for a long time, he will be too far removed for too long a time from the rugged life and challenges that he is to meet in the ministry.

When young people are educated away from their churches for long periods of time, that very education sometimes puts them out of touch with their communities. They return to their people with strange ideas and habits. They are not even the best teachers of the people from whose intellectual and spiritual lives they have been absent for so long. They no longer know how to answer their difficulties or respond to their needs. They are disconnected and out of touch with the people. The community has not grown with them, nor they with the community. They are now "outsiders," and only a few exceptional people can overcome that profound difficulty. This will be avoided if the emerging leaders maintain their life, relationships and ministry in the local church while they participate in an intense time of learning, experience and growth.

FROM THE FACTORY TO THE FAMILY

By moving from a centralized "factory" mentality to a pervasive "family" approach to leader development in the church, the following can be achieved:

- Flexibility. When it comes to leader development, "one size" does not fit all. Around the world, leaders from a vast diversity of cultures, backgrounds, experiences, education levels, etc., need to be built. Our approaches must be flexible and customizable. In addition, in many countries, the environment is rapidly changing around the church, again requiring flexibility in our approaches to leader development.
- Multiplication. The inherent limitations of the centralized factory will be lifted, the family approach providing a model

that can be multiplied virtually endlessly, with every local church or cluster of churches providing a learning environment for their emerging leaders.

- Self-support. The local church provides the financial support for the learning process, thus maintaining both responsibility for and control of the building of its own emerging leaders. To be truly self-governing, the community must be self-supporting.
- Holistic development. The learning process becomes considerably more effective because the local church provides the spiritual, relational and practical context for the development of the whole person.
- Security in restricted countries. In restricted countries, "factories" are obviously not viable due to their size, visibility and the ease with which they can be closed down. Church-integrated learning communities, on the other hand, can be small, easily-hidden and pervasive.
- The right people receive training. The emerging and existing leaders who need training the most are those who are already engaged in ministry and cannot leave their work for years at a time to go and study in a distant Bible school. In the traditional approach, we consistently train the wrong people.
- Ongoing, lifelong leader development. The training is not limited to a certain period of time, but continues throughout the emerging leaders' lives. Leaders are built over lifetimes!
- Effective evaluation. Members of the local community who know the emerging leader and who work with him on a daily basis are the very best ones to help him both establish goals for his development and evaluate his growth toward those goals.

NEW ROLES FOR THE OLD FACTORIES

It is conceivable that if a church denomination or network were to adopt a church-integrated learning community approach to leader development, this would not necessarily mean the end of their seminaries and

Bible schools; these entities could adopt new roles. In their new roles they would no longer do all the training *for* the churches; instead they would serve the churches as *they* build their own leaders. This support would involve the following areas:

- Envisioning and equipping local leaders to build leaders.
- Designing appropriate holistic processes and learning experiences to be used in the local learning communities.
- Developing appropriate materials and resources to be used in the local learning communities.
- Maintaining standards of training quality.
- Providing certain kinds of specialized learning.

This decentralized leader development with some measure of centralized support has a New Testament precedent. Clearly, the Jerusalem (Acts 8:14, 25; 15:4, 30-33), Ephesian (Acts 19:9-10) and Antioch churches (Acts 13:1-3; 15:36) served the churches around them in a variety of ways. In fact, this gave rise to the writing of most of the New Testament!

A STRATEGY TO IMPACT A NATION

To illustrate the above strategy, the following discussion concerns a hypothetical nation.

This nation has about 5000 churches. The current training is being done by 10 Bible schools with about 50 students each. The cost per student is about US$500 per year. This means that a total of 500 emerging leaders are being trained at a cost of US$250,000 per year.

While we rejoice that 500 emerging leaders are receiving training, this strategy has clear limitations:

- The training is largely academic, being disconnected from the local church environment. The whole person is not being built – a *quality* issue.

- There are not enough new leaders being trained – a *quantity* issue.
- Since the local churches are not directly involved in the training, they do not have a deep sense of ownership or responsibility. Consequently, it is hard for the Bible schools to fund their ongoing operations. Much of their funding comes from outside the country, and attached to that funding there are often "strings" (outside control and agendas).

However, if the local churches become the primary units of leader development, with the ongoing support of centralized envisioning-equipping-resourcing centers, the following can take place:

- If each local church will focus on building just *one* emerging leader, the numbers will increase dramatically. Now, *5000* emerging leaders are receiving training. Some churches can build two or three leaders; some can build ten or more! The crisis of quantity has been addressed.
- In the spiritual, relational and experiential context of the local churches, the leader development process can be considerably more holistic – character, spiritual life, marriage issues, practical ministry competencies, etc., can all be dealt with. The crisis of quality has been addressed.
- Since the training is based organically in the local churches, the cost is minimal. In addition, the local churches are now involved directly in the leader development so they have a much stronger sense of ownership and responsibility. Consequently, whatever costs are involved can be covered by the local churches. No outsiders are involved and the indigenous leaders remain in control of the training. The costs of the regional centers are also minimal and can be covered by the local churches who receive their help.

The following table summarizes the contrasts:

Contrasts between the Two Strategies	
Traditional Strategy	**ConneXions Strategy**
The local churches funnel their emerging leaders into the centralized Bible schools who do the training for them	A web of local churches around the nation that are the primary units of leader development, with equipping and resourcing from regional centers
500 students	5000+ emerging leaders
Largely academic training	Holistic leader development
Cost of US$250,000 per year	Minimal cost
Dependence on foreign funding (with possible "strings")	Owned and led by indigenous leaders
Some impact on the nation	Major impact on the nation

This is not to suggest that such a paradigm shift will be easy to accomplish. It is clear, however, that this strategy will meet the need. In addition, it has its roots in the New Testament.

CONCLUSION

In healthy leader development, the builder must work to create and sustain two kinds of community relationships for the emerging leaders in his care:

- Their relationships within the transformational, learning community itself.
- Their relationships within a larger spiritual community in which they live and serve.

If we can effectively do this – if we can move from the "factory" to the "family" in our leader development – we will dramatically increase both the numbers and the quality of the leaders we build.

Individually or in your team:

1. Please find examples of learning communities in which leaders were built. For example, David's "mighty men" (2 Samuel 23), the "company of the prophets" in the time of Elijah and Elisha, Jesus' twelve disciples, Paul's apostolic team, Paul's learning community in the lecture hall of Tyrannus (Acts 19:9). Please note some of the characteristics of these communities.

2. From the Scriptures, please demonstrate the importance of community in the life of a leader.

3. Suggest ways that a healthy relationship between a learning community and a local church or cluster of churches can be established and maintained. Please be specific and practical.

Leaders Build Leaders

While God is the ultimate One responsible for all leader development, and the entire church community is responsible for the holistic development of the leader, primary "hands-on" responsibility for building leaders resides in leaders.

> *He appointed twelve – designating them apostles – that they might be with him… (Mark 3:14)*

Mark 3:14 summarizes the first aspect of Jesus' primary method of building leaders: "that they might be with Him."

Leaders build leaders. By themselves, teachers don't build leaders, although they are an important part of the process.[16] By themselves, books, curriculum and courses don't build leaders, although they can help.[17] Just as hammers and saws do not build houses by themselves, books alone do not build leaders. It takes a leader to impart the vision, passion, courage and strategic perspectives of leadership.

Consequently, our process of leader development must not try to be a

---

[16] Here are the fundamental differences: *leaders* work with people, are oriented toward action and change and require fruit, while *teachers* work with ideas, are oriented toward learning and thinking, and *pastors* are oriented toward care-taking of the people. Certainly a man could function as both a leader and teacher, or as both a leader and pastor (or as a leader, teacher and pastor). The presence of all three functions is vital for the church as a whole to be healthy, but it is important for us to understand that the three functions are distinct. Please see *Leadership: SpiritBuilt Leadership #1* by Malcolm Webber for more on the essential nature of leadership.

[17] It would be both inaccurate and counterproductive to suggest that Jesus was against books and teaching tools. Even though He did not write any books or letters during His earthly ministry, He did inspire the entire Bible – the greatest Book ever written!

"package" that will work "all-by-itself." Packages don't build leaders; leaders build leaders. Our processes are only tools (hopefully good ones) that will work in the hands of a mature and qualified leader. The skill does not lie in the tool but in the hands of the craftsman. Additionally, we expect each leader to take the tool and use it differently, each according to his own unique situation, needs and style. The tool should never rule.

The traditional model has overemphasized the role of teachers, while underemphasizing the role of leaders. While we should use books, courses and training seminars, we should not rely exclusively on them. Leader development is accomplished best by leaders who personally work with the emerging leaders and give general oversight to the use of all other influences in their lives and ministries.

The Leader oversees it all
and gives personal
involvement.

The Leadership Toolkit:
Books, courses, curriculum,
seminars, exposure to other
leaders.

This was what Jesus did. Jesus formed His leaders personally. He called all His disciples by name (Matt. 10:1-4). He called them first to be "with Him."

> *He appointed twelve – designating them apostles – that they might be with him and that he might send them out to preach and to have authority to drive out demons. (Mark 3:14-15)*

In Jesus' day there were many Bible schools run by the religious leaders; Jesus ignored them all.

Leaders build leaders, and Jesus took personal responsibility for each of the leaders He built. He did not delegate this to some other training entity.

If leadership merely consisted of knowing a set of facts and mastering a few competencies, then the great task of building new leaders could be delegated to someone else. But leadership first consists of knowing God. And after that it involves issues such as proper relationships with others in a community of accountability, support and servanthood. Moreover, it involves deep and complex issues of character and personal calling, and knowing how to think conceptually and strategically. These are matters that cannot and must not be delegated to others. Only a leader who first has come to some level of personal maturity in these areas himself can lead another new leader into experiential maturity. These things do not come from books or seminars; they are only imparted from a leader who possesses them. These things cannot properly be taught in a classroom; they can only be shared in the context of life.

When you consider the most profound influences upon your own life, do you think of a book or a course, or do you remember a *person* (quite likely *people*) who impacted your life and ministry? The actual life experiences of most leaders confirm this biblical reality that leaders build leaders!

Of course, Jesus' disciples were not always physically present with Him. There were times when Jesus was alone with His Father (e.g., Mark 1:35) or ministering by Himself (e.g., John 4). There were also times when He sent His disciples away, giving them tasks that He knew would help them grow and mature (e.g., Luke 10:1). However, Jesus still personally designed the various transformational experiences He gave His disciples.

Thus, Jesus built His new leaders "with Him." Jesus' *personal influence* was what they became known for:

When they saw the courage of Peter and John and realized that they were unschooled, ordinary men, they were astonished and they took note that these men had been with Jesus. (Acts 4:13)[18]

They lived with Jesus, walked with Him, talked with Him, ate with Him, rested with Him and they watched Him in every situation. They saw how He lived, how He reacted, how He dealt with good people, how he dealt with bad people. They watched how He prayed to His Father, how He lived and ministered entirely out of the indwelling life of His Father. They watched Him heal the sick, cast out demons, miraculously feed the multitudes and raise the dead. They watched Him in victory; they watched Him experience the (apparent) defeat of His rejection and death on the cross. They watched Him cry over Jerusalem; they watched Him agonize over the hypocrisy of His people; they watched Him wrestle with the shortage of true laborers for the harvest. They saw how He exposed the false religious traditions of self-righteous men; they watched Him affirm the genuine purity and faith of the broken. They watched Him talk to God when things were going well and they watched Him pour out His heart to His Father as He struggled and "learned obedience" (Heb. 5:8).

Jesus built leaders who were "with Him." He did not do it at a distance; He did it closely, He did it personally. He did it properly.

THE PRIORITY OF LEADER DEVELOPMENT

Essentially, Jesus came to the earth to do three things: to die on the cross for the sins of humanity, to reveal the Father and proclaim the Kingdom of God by His words and works, and to build a small group of leaders. That's all He did!

In applying this to ourselves, thankfully, we do not have to die on the cross for humanity's sins, since Jesus has accomplished that once and for

---

[18] In contrast to our traditions, Jesus clearly did not deal much with academics. At the *end* of His training, His disciples were still "unschooled" (cf. John 7:14-16; 2 Cor. 11:6).

all. So we are left with only two core responsibilities – to do the ministry work and to build leaders. Sadly, many Christian leaders have been too busy with leadership to build leaders. We have, artificially and unbiblically, separated the two. While we have focused on proclaiming the Kingdom and revealing the Father – that is, doing the "ministry stuff" – we have rarely embraced personal and systematic responsibility for building leaders. Instead, we have sent our emerging leaders off to the "experts" in the remote academic institutions, hoping that they would do it for us.

Jesus did both. Moreover, He *always* did both. Every time He did ministry He took advantage of that opportunity to build leaders. Every time He built leaders, He accomplished ministry work at the same time. His example shows us that there is no better way to do ministry than by building leaders, and there is no better way to build leaders than by doing ministry.

We need to reconnect the two – leaders do ministry work *and* they build leaders at the same time.

In this biblical paradigm, leaders embrace personal responsibility for leader development as a core part of what it means to be a leader. This shift alone has the potential to address both issues of quality (as mature leaders impart the vision, passion, courage and strategic perspectives of leadership) and quantity (as every leader takes personal responsibility to build leaders).

HEARING AND SEEING

In the training of the twelve, both hearing and seeing the words and works of Christ were important (Luke 1:1-4; Matt. 13:16-17; Mark 4:34).

> *That which was from the beginning, which we have heard, which we have seen with our eyes, which we have looked at and our hands have touched – this we proclaim concerning the Word of life. (1 John 1:1)*

Jesus taught them His Word (Mark 4:34) and demonstrated to them the power of the kingdom (Matt. 11:4-5). It is not enough for leaders to teach the emerging leaders; they must also demonstrate what they are teaching.

Paul also taught his emerging leaders how to live both by his example and by his teaching:

> Whatever you have learned or received or heard from me, or seen in me – put it into practice... (Phil. 4:9)

> Join with others in following my example, brothers, and take note of those who live according to the pattern we gave you. (Phil. 3:17)

HOLISTIC DEVELOPMENT

Too often new leaders are trained in the mind, but not in the life of the Holy Spirit. We do not want a gap between the intellectual and spiritual development of the workers.

The builder must provide for the spiritual development of his prospective workers as well as their intellectual development. Jesus chose the disciples first of all that they might "be with Him" and only after that, should they preach the gospel and heal the sick.

> He appointed twelve – designating them apostles – that they might be with him and that he might send them out to preach and to have authority to drive out demons. (Mark 3:14-15)

Many times, He called His disciples apart for spiritual instruction. He took them with Him throughout His ministry, even to His cross and resurrection. After His resurrection they waited until they were filled with the Holy Spirit before they went "into all the world." Future leaders need more than theology, biblical surveys and church history; they must also learn the deeper meaning of the cross, the resurrection and the indwelling Spirit. Christian leaders, above all, must know God!

When they saw the courage of Peter and John and realized that they were unschooled, ordinary men, they were astonished and they took note that these men had been with Jesus. (Acts 4:13)

The builder must remember that his personal association with the new leaders is a vital factor in their training. Jesus took His disciples with Him.[19] In the normal course of life as the builder and new leaders spend time together, questions of all kinds will be brought up – doctrinal, social, ethical and personal. The new leaders will learn much from the builder's words, but more from his attitudes and actions. Through such contacts, the builder has the opportunity to impart not only his knowledge but also his own heart and vision.

Follow my example, as I follow the example of Christ. (1 Cor. 11:1)

At all times, the builder must be a spiritual example of a man who knows God and understands the moving of the Holy Spirit.

HOW LEADERS BUILD LEADERS

Leaders are not built in the classroom, but "on-the-job" as they deal with real problems and real opportunities, and face real consequences. Thus, deliberately building leaders is a truly complex challenge. If you ask leaders where they learned their leadership abilities, they will often tell you the two things that contributed the most were their experiences (both good and bad) and the leaders they have known and served (role

---

[19] Cf. Paul with Timothy (Acts 16:1-4; Rom. 16:21; 1 Cor. 4:17), Titus (2 Cor. 8:23; Gal. 2:1), Silas (Acts 15:40; 2 Cor. 1:19; 1 Thess. 1:1; 2 Thess. 1:1), and Aquila and Priscilla (Acts 18:2, 18-19; Rom. 16:3).

models with whom they have had direct personal contact).[20]

An effective leader develops other leaders through:

1. Taking personal responsibility for the deliberate and systematic building of other leaders – and not delegating it to others. All the great biblical leaders did this.

    This building will be both active and passive. *Active* leader development occurs when the builder deliberately creates transformational learning experiences for emerging leaders (e.g., Matt. 5–7; 25; Mark 4; 9:2-8; John 13:1-17).

    In *passive* building, the builder facilitates the best use of existing conditions or serendipitous spontaneous experiences for the emerging leaders (e.g., Matt. 8:23-27; 20:20-27; Mark 2:1-12; Luke 9:51-56).

2. Genuine relationships.

    Leaders build leaders in relationship. Leaders are not built by listening to lectures at school, but through vital relationships with leaders.

    Leadership is about people, and Jesus demonstrated the truly

---

[20] For example, one organization studied the impact of only training versus training with follow-up coaching. Thirty-one managers underwent a conventional managerial training program, which was followed by eight weeks of one-on-one executive coaching. The training alone increased their productivity by 22.4%. However, the coaching – which included goal setting, collaborative problem solving, practice, feedback, supervisory involvement, evaluation of end-results, and a public presentation – increased their productivity by 88%, a significantly greater gain compared to training alone. This study demonstrates the power of the relational dynamic even in secular managerial training. ("Executive coaching as a transfer of training tool: effects on productivity in a public agency" by Gerald Olivero, K. Denise Bane and Richard E. Kopelman. *Public Personnel Management*. December 22, 1997. Volume: 26 Issue: 4 Pages: 461-470.)

relational nature of leadership.

Jesus was not only "relational" in His leadership; He was *"truly* relational." He genuinely liked people. He *wanted* to spend time with people, listening to them, talking with them, helping them with their lives, leading them to the Father.

Apart from this genuine love for people, spiritual leadership soon becomes cold and lifeless, a mere going through the religious motions – a plastic and passionless professionalism.

Moreover, Jesus never *learned* to be relational; it came naturally to Him out of His union with His Father. In inward fellowship with His Father, Jesus knew His Father's love for people. He didn't just know about it as a doctrine from seminary – He *knew* His Father's love for people; He was absorbed in it, filled with it.

How often today we meet Christian leaders who merely "put up" with people because they have to. It's their job, and they have learned how to do it – yet they have no real heart for it. Today we are very good at producing leaders who are efficient "project managers": task-oriented achievers who can "get the job done" whatever it is – evangelism, pastoring, counseling, small groups, teaching. We are not so good at raising up leaders who genuinely love people.

Many times this lack of genuine concern in soul-winning causes unsaved people to react against those who would offer help. The unsaved seem to sense inwardly that the would-be evangelists are merely interested in them as pieces of merchandise to rescue from the fire. It is not out of any personal love for the sinner, but they have a command to obey, a ministry to perform, a project to accomplish. Such ministry is stiff, cold and impersonal.

We often see the same thing in pastoral ministry. The pastor has a fixed wooden smile for people, but in his heart there is no burning love. His answers are the "right" pat answers he has learned to give; they do not come spontaneously from a warm heart filled with the Father's love for His children. He promises to pray for the needy (and some even do go beyond the promise and think a quick thought of prayer or mouth a couple of words on their behalf), but his heart is not moved by their condition. This is professional leadership; it is a job that we accomplish well.

In contrast, Jesus' genuine warmth for His people can frequently be seen:

> O Jerusalem, Jerusalem...how often I have longed to gather your children together, as a hen gathers her chicks under her wings... (Luke 13:34)

> ...With fervent desire I have desired to eat this Passover with you... (Luke 22:15, NKJV)

> Greater love has no one than this, that he lay down his life for his friends... I no longer call you servants... Instead, I have called you friends... (John 15:13-15)

Jesus' desire to spend time with people – even the very "worst" of people – was seen in the religious leaders' angry rebuke:

> ...Here is... a friend of tax collectors and "sinners"... (Matt. 11:19)

Paul's love for people was the same: His heart broke over the condition of the churches he planted:

> My dear children, for whom I am again in the pains of childbirth until Christ is formed in you, (Gal. 4:19)

Paul genuinely loved them and cared about them. He was not putting up with them because it was his "job."

> *...you have such a place in our hearts that we would live or die with you. (2 Cor. 7:3)*

> *God can testify how I long for all of you with the affection of Christ Jesus. (Phil. 1:8)*

> *we were gentle among you, like a mother caring for her little children. We loved you so much that we were delighted to share with you not only the gospel of God but our lives as well, because you had become so dear to us. (1 Thess. 2:7-8)*

> *For what is our hope, or joy, or crown of rejoicing? Are not even ye in the presence of our Lord Jesus Christ at his coming? (1 Thess. 2:19)*

> *For now we live, if you stand fast in the Lord. For what thanks can we render to God for you, for all the joy with which we rejoice for your sake before our God, (1 Thess. 3:8-9, NKJV)*

> *Recalling your tears, I long to see you, so that I may be filled with joy. (2 Tim. 1:4)*

This last verse reveals a fervent personal love that was mutual between Paul and Timothy. Timothy cried when parting with Paul; Paul anticipated great joy at their reunion. This depth of intimacy and sensitivity shows that Paul resisted the hardness and negativity that too often marks those who have had the most extensive experience in the "hard knocks" of ministry.

Today, many leaders are confused about the nature of ministry. Such a leader sees "ministry" as something that needs to be accomplished and developed; in his mind, his "ministry" has come to have an existence separate and distinct from the people he says he serves. He loves ministry but he is bored and irritated by people. Biblically, however, we do not develop and serve "ministries," we love and serve people. Our people are not simply a means to the end of "ministry"; the people God has called us to lead *are our end!* This was the life Jesus lived before His disciples; this was the example He gave them. This was how He built them – through His own genuine relationship with them.

3. Openly sharing their lives.

There are many biblical examples of leaders openly sharing their lives, their inner motives, thoughts, fears, struggles, hardships, victories, etc. with their disciples.

Paul, for example, frequently shared from his heart:

> *We do not want you to be uninformed, brothers, about the hardships we suffered in the province of Asia. We were under great pressure, far beyond our ability to endure, so that we despaired even of life. Indeed, in our hearts we felt the sentence of death. But this happened that we might not rely on ourselves but on God, who raises the dead. He has delivered us from such a deadly peril, and he will deliver us. On him we have set our hope that he will continue to deliver us, as you help us by your prayers. Then many will give thanks on our behalf for the gracious favor granted us in answer to the prayers of many. (2 Cor. 1:8-11; see also Acts 20:22-24; Rom. 7:7-25; 1 Cor. 4:11-13; 2 Cor. 6:3-10; 11:5-12, 21-33; 12:1-10; Phil. 3:4-10, 13-14; 4:10-20)*

Throughout Scripture, it is the *personal reality* of someone's life – not just courses on theoretical subjects – that encourages us and teaches us how to trust God and walk with Him (e.g., Ps. 51; Jam. 5:10-11, 17-18).

Effective leaders are passionate people who deliberately generate positive emotional energy in others through their personal one-on-one relationships with them. Through their examples, they teach others how to think. Through their experiences, they model faith. They also demonstrate spiritual "guts" – the willingness and ability to face reality and make tough decisions.

They embody their ideas and values in living stories. They tell stories about their past experiences to explain what they have learned, their convictions and their vision. They create stories about the future of the church and its leaders. They move others, both emotionally and intellectually, to pursue the future they describe.

> *You, however, know all about my teaching, my way of life, my purpose, faith, patience, love, endurance, perse-cutions, sufferings – what kinds of things happened to me in Antioch, Iconium and Lystra, the persecutions I endured. Yet the Lord rescued me from all of them. In fact, everyone who wants to live a godly life in Christ Jesus will be persecuted, while evil men and impostors will go from bad to worse, deceiving and being deceived. But as for you, continue in what you have learned and have become convinced of, because you know those from whom you learned it, (2 Tim. 3:10-14)*

Thus, leaders and teachers should not merely teach courses, but they must share their lives with their emerging leaders.

When you think of people who have deeply touched your life, what do you remember: theoretical courses they taught you or the experiences of their lives they shared with you with tears?

4. Teaching the Word of God.

As noted, in 2 Timothy 3:10-14, Paul shares from his life. Then in verses 15-17, he refers to the Scriptures:

> *and how from infancy you have known the holy Scriptures, which are able to make you wise for salvation through faith in Christ Jesus. All Scripture is God-breathed and is useful for teaching, rebuking, correcting and training in righteousness, so that the man of God may be thoroughly equipped for every good work. (2 Tim. 3:15-17)*

The combination of personal experiences and the Scriptures is a powerful way that leaders bring transformation to others.

> *Remember your leaders, who spoke the word of God to you. Consider the outcome of their way of life and imitate their faith. Jesus Christ is the same yesterday and today and forever. (Heb. 13:7-8)*

5. Exposure to other leaders – both good (Phil. 3:17; 2 Tim. 3:10-11) and bad (2 Tim. 3:8-9).[21]

> *Therefore I urge you to imitate me. For this reason I am sending to you Timothy, my son whom I love, who is faithful in the Lord. He will remind you of my way of life in Christ Jesus, which agrees with what I teach everywhere in every church. (1 Cor. 4:16-17)*

From these examples, emerging leaders will learn many positive things such as:

- compassion
- integrity

---

[21] We can learn from bad leaders as well as from good ones. Sometimes, we will learn more from a bad leader than a good one!

- ethics
- how to treat people
- how to accept responsibility
- how to make tough decisions
- how to involve others
- how to motivate people
- how to recognize the accomplishments of others
- how to delegate
- confidence in others
- how to learn from one's failures
- how to work with organizational politics
- how to perform the leadership "balancing acts":
  - acting alone *and* working with others
  - making tough decisions *and* treating people with compassion
  - having the confidence to act *and* the humility to know there are other views
  - seizing opportunities *and* planning for the future
  - taking control *and* accepting the will of God
  - persevering in the face of adversity, *yet* changing direction when you're wrong

These are all abilities that will *only* be learned "on-the-job" in real-life situations, in relationships with more mature leaders.

6. While the most powerful form of building occurs in face-to-face active relationships with leaders, it is still beneficial to expose emerging leaders to multiple leaders, both good and bad, through reading or hearing about them ("passive mentoring").

7. Some other ways that leaders can develop leaders are:

   a. Allowing an individual to observe the inner workings of a ministry (particularly in the area of the leader's calling) by inviting him into the action (e.g., Matt. 3:14; 17:1-3; 26:36-40). Of course, there is a balance here.

Sometimes they should not see the inner workings because they may, for example, lack sufficient maturity. In addition, they should be highly trusted first. But, leaders should take people with them and let them see what is really happening.

b. Buffering the person from the system, allowing him some room to make mistakes (Matt. 17:14-21; Luke 22:31-32).

c. Being willing to admit mistakes and show their vulnerabilities, in order to serve as effective role models for others (Phil. 3:4-14).

d. Modeling and encouraging reflection on the experiences of their lives (Phil. 3:4-14).

e. Proactively encouraging and facilitating mentoring relationships with other leaders (2 Tim. 2:2).

f. Occasionally getting the person's attention through reprimand, punishment or warning (Mark 8:33).

g. Alternating tough and supportive action, as it is appropriate (Mark 16:14-18; 1 Cor. 1:4-8 with 3:1-3; Gal. 1:6; 3:1-3 with 5:10; Col. 1:2-6 with 2:20-23).

These are some of the specific ways through which leaders build leaders. Fundamentally, development involves providing opportunities, opportunities for:

- learning
- study
- teaching and training others
- experience
- responsibilities
- relationships
- observing
- suffering

Of course, there are no guarantees that specific individuals will take advantage of those opportunities, just as possessing certain leadership gifts or traits is no guarantee that one will emerge as a leader. One must personally be motivated to lead, and to learn and grow as a leader. Many people simply do not want the responsibilities and hardships of leadership. Nevertheless, without these opportunities there will be little development; the greatest of all potentials will be wasted!

THE ROLES OF THE BUILDER

There are several distinct "hats" that a leader will wear in his relationship with an emerging leader. There are many areas of overlap but each practice has its own character relating to content, process and purpose.

	Training	**Counseling**	**Confronting**	**Mentoring**
Content	Technical skills	Personal problems	Negative attitudes or actions	Relationships with God & with one's community
Process	Competencies	Personal growth issues	Deal with character problems	Development of spiritual and life issues
Purpose	Establish and meet goals & objectives	Physical, mental, emotional & spiritual health	Overcome substandard performance or persistent concerns	Recognize and fulfill one's life purpose in God

First, a leader-builder will be a Trainer. Training is the instructional process by which specific knowledge and skills are transferred to the emerging leader. It usually occurs early in the relationship with a more experienced leader. Training also occurs at any time when new skills are required. It is an ongoing and never-ending process of continually improving the "technical" capacities of the new leader, so that he knows what he is doing.

Second, at times the builder will be a Counselor. Counseling is helping people who have personal or interpersonal issues – inside or outside of their work or ministry responsibilities – that are interfering with their ability to properly function.

Third, it will occasionally be necessary to be a Confronter. Confronting is how we deal with negative attitudes, disruptive behaviors or substandard performance. Goals and objectives must be clarified and the emerging leader helped to move toward positive solutions. Underlying character or spiritual issues may also need to be dealt with.

Finally, the leader-builder will be a Mentor. Mentoring is the process in which one leader shares his wisdom, his experience and his life with emerging leaders on a one-on-one basis. He helps the new leader with his relationships with God and with others, and he assists him in understanding his overall life's purposes in God and how those purposes relate to his current situation. He also helps facilitate the emerging leader's personal networking, and provides comfort when the emerging leader feels overwhelmed. The new leader learns by the example and personal influence of the more experienced one.

Clearly, to build new leaders properly requires a significant personal investment of time, as well as emotional and spiritual energy!

PRACTICAL IMPLICATIONS FOR BUILDERS

First, any learning community that we initiate must be built on leaders and communities, and not on curriculum, books or courses. Before we begin the learning community, we must find the right leader in the right community. Finding the necessary curriculum – as important as it is – is only a secondary issue. The curriculum is only a tool in the hands of the craftsman. A good craftsman can make even a poor tool work successfully; while a perfect tool is useless without the craftsman.

Our goal, of course, is to have great craftsmen with great tools! But our traditional paradigm of teaching and learning emphasizes the tools – the curriculum, the books and the courses – while not paying sufficient attention to the craftsmen. Sad to say, many professors in many training institutions have had little successful experience in practical leadership themselves, and rely on books and curriculum. This is a situation – and a mindset – that must be changed.

In the traditional paradigm, when a man comes to a new area and wants to build leaders, he first looks for a building and then brings his curriculum in and gets started. In a healthier approach, however, he first looks for a leader within a community to work with. Too many times the long-term fruit of the old paradigm is empty shells of buildings, while the long-term fruit of leaders building leaders is changed lives and effective ministries.

Second, the combination of gifting – leadership and teaching – is a very good mix to lead a learning community. In addition, the more leaders who are involved in the learning community, the better. That way the emerging leaders are exposed to many different perspectives on life and leadership.

Third, God puts leaders with leaders to build them. As we seek Him, God arranges circumstances for us to grow ourselves and for us to help others grow. This means that you may not be the right person to build a particular leader. We must seek God concerning who He wants to work with us and who He wants us to work with. Moreover, an emerging leader will often do better with a leader who has the same (or, at least, similar) ultimate calling.

Type of Relationship	Purpose	Best One To Do It
Discipling	Foundation	Any believer can do it.
Mentoring	Formation	One with a similar calling is most effective.
Coaching	Facilitation	One with wisdom and broad life and ministry experience is best.

Finally, as we have observed, the sharing of life is a central responsibility of the builder. That is what impacts emerging leaders. Leaders and teachers must do more than merely teach through a prescribed course; they must share their hearts and lives with their growing leaders.

THE "CHICKEN OR THE EGG" QUESTION

As he teaches this principle in various nations, the author is frequently asked the question, "This principle of 'leaders build leaders' is obviously a biblical one, but what do we do if we don't have any healthy leaders to begin with?"

This is the classic "chicken or the egg" question. So, which one does come first? The answer is very simple: Which one do you have? That's the one that comes first.

In other words, you may not have multitudes of entirely healthy leaders who can then build emerging leaders. But who do you have? Who can you get? The situation will rarely be optimal. You've got to start somewhere, so start with what you have. Just start!

CONCLUSION

If we can successfully change our thinking on this issue – if we can reconnect a leader's responsibility to do leadership work with his responsibility to build leaders – the fruit will be considerable improvement in both the quality and the quantity of our emerging leaders.

Individually or in your study group:

1. Please find biblical examples of leaders who took personal responsibility for building new leaders.

2. Please find biblical examples of the effects of personal relationships with leaders on emerging leaders.

3. Please find biblical examples of emerging leaders being exposed to bad leadership. What were the positive effects of this?

4. From Jesus' ministry, please find examples of both *active* and *passive* leader development. *Active* building occurs when the builder deliberately creates transformational learning opportunities for emerging leaders. In *passive* building, the builder facilitates the best use of existing conditions or serendipitous spontaneous experiences for the emerging leader.

5. Please find examples from Paul's ministry where he actively shared his life with the people he was building.

6. Please find biblical examples of leaders using the following as they built emerging leaders:
    a. Allowing the emerging leader to see the inner workings of the ministry.
    b. Giving the emerging leader "room" to make mistakes.
    c. Admitting their own personal mistakes and showing vulnerability.
    d. Modeling and encouraging reflection on the experiences of their lives and ministries.
    e. Facilitating mentoring relationships with other leaders.
    f. Using reprimand, punishment or warning.
    g. Alternating tough and supportive action.

The Builder Himself

Leaders who build leaders should themselves be involved in the daily responsibilities of leadership. They should not teach in some artificial environment removed from the real world, as is common in traditional Bible schools and seminaries. Jesus and Paul both conducted extensive and fruitful personal ministries while concurrently building new leaders.

This practice:

- Maintains integrity. The builder is not teaching theory but reality. It works: he is living it and doing it. This is quite different from traditional schools, concerning which it is said, "Those who can, do; those who cannot, teach."
- Brings credibility. The leader actually has practiced what he is teaching. He genuinely knows what he is talking about. He is able to show emerging leaders fruit, and not only seeds.
- Maintains reality and balance in ministry. You tend more toward practical things and not theoretical, abstract issues when you are personally and daily involved in the struggles of genuine leadership and ministry. In an artificial environment, the teachers get out of touch, as well as the students.
- Brings empathy. The teacher is facing the same kind of struggles his students face.
- Increases effectiveness. Each activity enhances the other.

This becomes a rigorous lifestyle for the builder, as he juggles the various responsibilities of leadership as well as building. He must be careful to teach only what he really needs to personally teach, instead of trying to do everything that the traditional model suggests is necessary. In addition, he must let others also contribute to the process. Having the community helps greatly here – providing other teachers and mentors, as well as those who pray for, nurture and encourage the emerging leaders.

A leader who accepts the challenge of building new leaders must be careful to maintain balance in his own life. In Jesus' ministry, we see a wonderful balance. He spent much time building leaders (e.g., Mark 3:14), but He also spent personal one-on-one time with "ordinary" people (e.g., John 4:7ff). Jesus did not withdraw from "ordinary" people and only focus on the "more important" leaders He was building. Keeping this balance helps us to:

- Genuinely care for people.
- Stay in touch with people.
- Maintain perspective on the real issues of life.
- Discipline our lives to accomplish every task of leadership, not just one or two of the "most important ones."

Here are some biblical examples of leaders who continued their own ministries while building new leaders:

- Jesus and the Twelve.
- Paul and his learning community in Ephesus (Acts 19:9-12).
- Paul and his apostolic team.
- Barnabas and Mark (Acts 15:39).
- John the Baptist and his disciples.
- Moses and Joshua.
- Eli and Samuel.
- Samuel and the company of the prophets.
- Elisha and his prophets.

Individually or in your study group:

1. Please find and discuss biblical examples of leaders who continued their ministries while building new leaders – in both testaments.

2. Please find biblical examples of leaders who maintained the balance of relationship with leaders and with "ordinary" people.

Leaders Are Built a Few at a Time

He told them another parable: "The kingdom of heaven is like a mustard seed, which a man took and planted in his field. Though it is the smallest of all your seeds, yet when it grows, it is the largest of garden plants and becomes a tree, so that the birds of the air come and perch in its branches." (Matt. 13:31-32)

When we look around at the world, we can easily be overwhelmed by the size of the need. Yet, today there are 682 million "Great Commission Christians" out of a world population of 6.4 billion people.[22] In other words, approximately 1 in 9 human beings alive on the earth is a "Great Commission Christian." This means that God really doesn't need you or me or our ministries. He has hundreds of thousands of churches and ministries around the world, and hundreds of millions of sons and daughters who can do the job for Him. If you or I disappeared tomorrow, it is not likely that the cause of the Kingdom would suffer too much!

However, what was the situation when Jesus walked the earth 2000 years ago? How many "Great Commission Christians" were there then? Arguably, only one – Jesus! Thus, Jesus had no option; He *had* to succeed. The future of the Kingdom of God *entirely* depended on Him! No one else could do it. If He failed, it was all over. Can you imagine the pressure He was under?

Here is the contrast. We are overwhelmed by the need around us and our thoughts are usually along the lines of: "The need is so great we have to train thousands of leaders! How can we set up a 'production line' of some kind so that we can produce the multitudes of necessary leaders quickly?" The truth is that whether we live or die does not affect the ultimate success of God's plan – in reality, it does not. But when Jesus looked at a much greater need, instead of thinking of production lines

---

[22] Source: Center for the Study of Global Christianity (mid-2004).

He chose twelve men and concentrated on them for three years! That was His response to the incredible need that He faced.[23]

Surely we can learn from His example that it is far better to do a lot with few, than a little with many. In response to a far greater crisis of lack of leadership than we will ever face, Jesus' focus was not on numbers, but on quality. He did it right! Jesus concentrated on building only a few leaders. He built only twelve main leaders who would head His entire organization that would change the world! This was the model He gave us.

Since leaders personally build leaders, one leader can build only a *few* other leaders at a time – that is, if he wants to do it properly. He cannot personally build thousands of leaders. As much as we might like to flatter ourselves that we can build thousands of leaders, it would be wise for us to remember that Jesus built only a handful and it took Him three years to do it!

The Lord Jesus Christ was the greatest Builder of leaders who has ever lived, and He focused on a few. His vision was huge; His vision was a church that would eventually number in the hundreds of millions! His vision was the taking of the gospel of the Kingdom of God to all nations! Yet He focused on a few men – twelve to be exact. Twelve men to change the world. Twelve men to whom He would commit the monumental task of building His church. And one of them failed, leaving Him only eleven in the end! With these few men He spent much of His time; into these few men He poured His life; to these few men He committed His entire future agenda for the world.

---

[23] Significantly, Jesus' ultimate vision was to establish hundreds of thousands of local churches around the world (as part of one unified Church), and yet, personally, He didn't plant a single one! He built leaders who planted churches. This is not to suggest that we shouldn't plant churches. The point is: we have done it the other way around, by multiplying evangelistic efforts and planting many churches and then trying to address the need for leaders. We must raise healthy leader development to the same level of priority and focus as church planting. This is the only way we will plant and grow sustainable churches.

And did Jesus' strategy succeed? Today's 682 million "Great Commission Christians" are proof that it did indeed succeed!

From this we can learn that when it comes to building leaders, it is better to be deeply committed to building a few great leaders than to be under-committed to building many mediocre ones. This is such a hard lesson for us to learn. Overwhelmed by the admittedly huge task before us, we repeatedly attempt to set up spiritual "production lines" to turn out leaders by the thousand. Too often, unfortunately, the leaders we turn out are under-built, still entangled in the unresolved struggles of their pasts, not sufficiently grounded in either the Word or the Spirit of God, not sure of who they are or what they're to do, and not really competent to do it anyway.

Leadership building does not happen on a production line. It is far better to build a few leaders right, than to build many leaders poorly.

Paul and other biblical leaders pursued leader development the same way. The idea of *personally* and *quickly* raising up "thousands of leaders" is not a biblical one. The biblical model is more like this: "the things you have heard me say in the presence of many witnesses entrust to reliable men who will also be qualified to teach others" (2 Tim. 2:2). In other words, build a few good leaders, who in turn will each build a few good leaders, who will each do the same, and so on. In a relatively short time, we will have the dramatic multiplication of leaders we need. The difference is: they will be *good* leaders. This is the "mustard seed" principle: the small seed becomes a large, fruitful tree.

We must not allow the overwhelming size and urgency of the great task ahead of us (e.g., "the whole world needs to be reached!") and an exaggerated sense of our own capacities or importance in this regard to dictate sloppy and insufficient approaches to leadership building. We must do what is necessary to build *good* leaders. Forget the production line! Let's do it right!

We must lay down our "production line" mentality, which is often driven by our prideful desire to be known for having done something "big."

God's ways are not our ways. We desire greatness in the eyes of man. Let us instead seek greatness only in the eyes of God. Let us pursue the obscurity of reality rather than the fame of superficiality.

The American scholar Henry Adams wrote,

> The difference is slight, to the influence of an author, whether he is read by five hundred readers, or by five hundred thousand. If he can select the five hundred, he reaches the five hundred thousand.

Gideon defeated the Midianites with only 300 (Jud. 7), but they were the right 300!

The Kingdom of God "is like a mustard seed, which is the smallest seed you plant in the ground. Yet when planted, it grows and becomes the largest of all garden plants, with such big branches that the birds of the air can perch in its shade" (Mark 4:31-32). This is how we will influence the lives of multitudes: through the obscurity of reality.

JESUS BUILT A FEW LEADERS

Jesus concentrated on building only a few leaders. Moreover, He intentionally *varied* the relationships that He had with them according to their future callings. We will now consider the different groups of emerging leaders who enjoyed various levels or depths of relationship with Jesus, the nature of their relationships, and the results.

Starting with those furthest from Christ, after the multitudes there were the 70:

> *After these things the Lord appointed seventy others also, and sent them two by two before His face into every city and place where He Himself was about to go. (Luke 10:1, NKJV)*

We could call this group, Jesus' "extended team" of leaders. They received

His basic teaching, they learned from watching His personal example, and they were directly commissioned by Him to their ministries. These 70 disciples accomplished extensive ministry on Jesus' behalf (Luke 10:1-20).

Then there were the Twelve:

> *When morning came, he called his disciples to him and chose twelve of them, whom he also designated apostles: (Luke 6:13)*

We might call this group, Jesus' "core leadership team." Along with everything the 70 disciples received, the twelve apostles were given additional special attention by Jesus. They received special teaching, revelation and disclosure (e.g., Matt. 20:17; Mark 9:35), special experiences (e.g., Mark 14:17ff; Luke 9:1-4, 12-17; John 6:67; Acts 1; 1 Cor. 15:5) and personal communication and fellowship with Jesus (Mark 3:14). This group of twelve (minus Judas, of course) became the top leadership team of the entire church (e.g., Acts 6:2, 4).

Then, within the group of twelve apostles, were the three: Peter, James and John. In addition to all the teaching and developmental experiences that the twelve apostles were given, the three also received some additional personal experiences that were profoundly transformational. Mark makes special mention of their calling (Mark 1:16-20[24]). They were with Jesus when He was glorified on the Mount of Transfiguration (Matt. 17:1-9), when He raised Jairus' daughter from the dead (Mark 5:37-43) and when He wrestled with the agony of His upcoming crucifixion in the Garden (Mark 14:33-34).[25] These three men were Jesus' intimate friends, His confidants. In a special way, they shared both His joys (e.g., on the Mount of Transfiguration) and His struggles (e.g., in the Garden[26]).

---

[24] Andrew is also included here.

[25] In Mark 13:3ff, Jesus shared some private revelation regarding the Last Days with the 3 along with Andrew.

[26] Because they were His friends, Jesus was genuinely grieved when they let Him down.

As a result of their special preparation, within Jesus' top leadership team, these three men became the key leaders of the church. Significantly, the three are all named by Paul in Galatians 2:9-10 as being the "pillars" of the Jerusalem church in the early days. James was no doubt the main leader of the early church in Jerusalem. Peter became the "apostle to the Jews" (Gal. 2:8), preached the message on the day of Pentecost that resulted in the first major harvest of souls (Acts 2) and was the first apostle to officially share the gospel with the Gentiles (Acts 10).

Finally, Jesus had His closest, most intimate relationship with John. John was Jesus' very intimate friend. John was with Jesus, along with Peter and James, during Jesus' special joys and struggles, but John enjoyed an even closer relationship with his Lord. As "the disciple whom Jesus loved" (John 13:23; 19:26; 20:2; 21:7, 20) John laid his head on Jesus' chest (John 13:23)!

What was the result of such a close relationship? Arguably, John became Jesus' "successor." Certainly no mere mortal could ever truly succeed Jesus in the absolute sense, but John had a very special ministry after Jesus' Ascension. John assumed responsibility for Jesus' mother after His crucifixion (John 19:25-27). He enjoyed the longest ministry of all the apostles, and he wrote the most and, possibly, the deepest writings. In a special way, John's writings reveal the Person of Jesus Christ as God, as well as the nature of the Christian life as union with God. In many ways, John was Jesus' "successor."

So, we see that Jesus had one successor, three intimate friends, twelve core leaders and an extended leadership team of 70. He worked with a handful, intensively with a few, and intimately with one.

Who	Their Role	Christ's Relationship with Them	Future Results
The multitudes, crowds	Received ministry	More distant ministry	Broad influence
The 70	Extended group of leaders	Basic teaching. Example. Model. Personally commissioned by Christ	Extensive ministry
The 12	Key leadership team	Special teaching. Special attention. Special experiences. Personal communication and fellowship with Christ. (plus everything noted above)	Overall leaders of *entire* church (core team)
The 3 Peter, James & John	Intimate friends. Confidants. Shared joys (e.g., Mount of Transfiguration), and struggles (e.g., Garden of Gethsemane)	Special personal events. (plus everything noted above)	James was the key leader of first church; therefore, he was slain by Herod. Peter was the apostle to the Jews; he was used mightily at Pentecost; he brought the gospel to the Gentiles (Acts 10). Gal. 2:8-9. John – see below
The 1 John	"Successor."[27] Intimate friend	Intimate friend. Head on bosom. Disciple whom Jesus "loved." (plus everything noted above)	Longest ministry. Wrote more. Wrote deeper. Wrote regarding the Person of Christ & nature of the Christian life more. Took responsibility for Jesus' mother

Now, let's look at the practical implications of this model for us.

PRACTICAL IMPLICATIONS FOR BUILDERS

1. Jesus varied the relationships that He had with His followers. He did this intentionally to develop the various kinds and levels of future leaders He needed. When He called these men, His calls were made in view of the end purpose He had in mind for them. He knew what they were going to do in the future and adjusted His building strategy and relationships accordingly. He did this intentionally; we should, too. One cannot build dozens of successors, only one. One cannot have scores of intimate friends, only a few. One should not have a top leadership team of hundreds, only about a dozen.

2. It would be appropriate in our situations, for leaders at *many* levels in an organization to follow this model to some extent.

3. The exact numbers are not the point, although they should be fairly close. You might have two or four intimate friends, but you will not have twenty.

4. The top levels of future leaders that we pick must be the right ones. There is no room for error regarding their callings in God. This is why Jesus spent so much time in prayer before calling His leaders in the first place (Luke 6:12-13). If anyone could have chosen the right ones without much trouble, it was He. But He could not afford a mistake. He only had three years; He couldn't do it twice. Neither can we! We must choose slowly and carefully.

5. This is not only a developmental model but also an effective long-term leadership structure.

---

[27] Obviously no one could be Jesus' successor in an absolute sense! But as much as Jesus could have a successor, John was it.

6. In Jesus' model we also see the intensely personal nature of leader development – particularly at the higher levels. Jesus did not have a merely formal, professional relationship with the leaders He was building. He was not a professor; He was a "friend" (John 15:14-15). This was how Jesus built a leadership team that changed the world.

7. If we focus on a few, inevitably there will be envy and competition from those not chosen. If Jesus experienced this (e.g., Matt. 20:20-21, 24), we will not avoid it. Jesus, of course, dealt with this head-on (Matt. 20:25-28); He did not politely ignore it.

   We must make sure, however, that we do not parade "the chosen few" before the rest – or let them parade themselves. Instead, we should deliberately seek an appropriate measure of hiddenness and obscurity in our dealings with "our few." This will help them avoid the mixed motives and debilitating pride of elitism.

8. The fact that leaders are built a few at a time does not mean we cannot build many leaders quickly. Leaders build leaders; consequently, many leaders can build many leaders.

   In summary, leaders are built a few at a time, and our relationships with that few need to vary intentionally.

Individually or in your study group:

1. Please find biblical examples of leaders who focused on building a small number of future leaders.

2. Honestly examine your own heart. What is your motivation for wanting to be known for having personally raised up "thousands of leaders"?

3. Prayerfully determine: who are "the few" that you will focus on?

We Must Build the Right Ones!

Since a leader can personally build only a few new leaders, he must be sure that he builds the right ones. He must prayerfully and carefully choose the right few. Unfortunately, too often we spend more time trying to train people than we do making sure we are training the right people in the first place. For most people, formal development programs will not automatically transform them into superior leaders, as if they were butterflies emerging from cocoons. We should spend more time on accurately identifying which ones we should work with.

Today, many Christian training institutions will accept almost anyone who applies, as long as they can pay the tuition. In contrast, biblical leaders did not simply hand out application forms, but they personally chose the people they would work with:

> As Jesus walked beside the Sea of Galilee, he saw Simon and his brother Andrew casting a net into the lake, for they were fishermen. "Come, follow me," Jesus said, "and I will make you fishers of men." At once they left their nets and followed him. When he had gone a little farther, he saw James son of Zebedee and his brother John in a boat, preparing their nets. Without delay he called them, and they left their father Zebedee in the boat with the hired men and followed him. (Mark 1:16-20)

No volunteer ever made it into the small community around Jesus. All were chosen. This was also true of Paul's learning community:

> He came to Derbe and then to Lystra, where a disciple named Timothy lived, whose mother was a Jewess and a believer, but whose father was a Greek. The brothers at Lystra and Iconium spoke well of him. Paul wanted to take him along on the journey... (Acts 16:1-3)

Potential leaders are more available than many people think. The difficulty is to identify them properly, and doing so requires sorting through a myriad of nuances and subtleties of healthy leadership.

So, how can we know who to build? How can we discern the call of God upon a person's life? These are common questions in leaders' minds. The following are some guidelines concerning how to choose the right emerging leaders to work with.

1. Look beyond appearances and be willing to take some risks.

   In choosing His key leaders, Jesus looked for men of character (John 1:47) and spiritual passion (Mark 1:18, 20). They all forsook everything to follow Him (Matt. 19:27). However, at the same time, they were ignorant, narrow-minded, super-stitious, and full of prejudices, misconceptions and animos-ities (John 1:46; Matt. 14:26; 20:21, 24; Luke 9:49, 52-54; Acts 4:13). Jesus knew they could grow.

   In choosing His leaders, Jesus disregarded social convention and human wisdom. For example, in choosing Matthew, Jesus chose one of the hated tax-collectors who could not fail to be a stumbling block to the Jews, and would, therefore, be a source of weakness rather than of strength to Him. Moreover, when Jesus invited Simon the Zealot to follow Him, He embraced an unsafe man who might make Him an object of political suspicion.

   Jesus was not afraid of the drawbacks arising out of the external connections or the past history of His emerging leaders. Confident in the power of the truth He knew He would give them, He was entirely indifferent to all such worries, choosing the base things of the world in preference to the honorable. Furthermore, Jesus wanted to gain followers from all classes of people (including the despised and dangerous) and so

He needed to have such classes represented among His key leadership team.[28]

2. Do not be in a hurry.

Do not be hasty in the laying on of hands (i.e., in choosing and appointing new leaders)... (1 Tim. 5:22)

Jesus' twelve arrived at their final intimate relationships with Him in three stages:

a. They believed in Jesus as the Messiah and were His occasional companions at convenient times.
b. They entirely, or at least partly, left their occupations to be with Him in uninterrupted fellowship.[29]
c. Jesus chose them from the multitude of His followers and formed them into a group to be trained as His future key leaders. This last event probably did not occur until all the twelve had been with Jesus for some time. He did not rush them into serious apprenticeship.

3. Pray much before the choice is made.

If Jesus needed to pray about making the right choices, how much more do we? Before Jesus chose His emerging leaders, He spent an entire night in prayer:

---

[28] It is also true that, in one sense, Jesus had to be content with fishermen, tax-collectors and zealots for His leaders. They were the best that could be had. The present leaders in society boasted of their unbelief (John 7:48). A few prominent men believed in Him but they were not passionate enough to be eligible for key leadership. For example, Nicodemus was timid in speaking on His behalf (John 7:50-51) and Joseph of Arimathea was a disciple "secretly because he feared the Jews" (John 19:38).

[29] For example, Matthew left his occupation entirely, while the fishermen probably did not do so.

One of those days Jesus went out to a mountainside to pray,
and spent the night praying to God. When morning came,
he called his disciples to him and chose twelve of them,
whom he also designated apostles... (Luke 6:12-13)

Jesus chose the men His Father led Him to. He chose the men
He saw in prayer.

...I tell you the truth, the Son can do nothing by himself;
he can do only what he sees his Father doing, because
whatever the Father does the Son also does. (John 5:19)

If there was ever a man who could simply look at people and
immediately know if they're the right ones, it was Jesus; yet He
spent the entire night in prayer.

Furthermore, if there was ever a leader who could have taken
the *wrong* person and made a good leader out of him, it was
Jesus; yet He spent the entire night in prayer. Jesus knew He
had to choose the right ones. He only had three years; if He
chose the wrong ones He would not get a second chance.

Today, sadly, we are frequently more concerned about filling
quotas and other complex financial issues than we are about
spending the necessary time in seeking God.

Leader development requires an intensive relationship
between the community and the emerging leaders. It requires
a deep commitment of time, resources, focus and energy – we
must choose the right ones, and only God can show us who
they are.

4. Consider the fruit of their existing leadership.

The past can be a good predictor of the future.

The brothers at Lystra and Iconium spoke well of him (i.e. Timothy). Paul wanted to take him along on the journey, so he circumcised him because of the Jews who lived in that area, for they all knew that his father was a Greek. (Acts 16:2-3)

In Acts 16, Paul recognized that Timothy, who had likely been saved during Paul's first visit to this area about four years earlier (Acts 14), had a fruitful and extensive ministry that involved at least two cities, Lystra and Iconium. Moreover, it appears there was unity among the brothers in these cities. The ability to bring unity between groups of believers is an apostolic characteristic. Paul observed all this and chose Timothy to travel with him.

5. Examine the recommendation of those around them.

The brothers at Lystra and Iconium spoke well of him. Paul wanted to take him along on the journey... (Acts 16:2-3; cf. 6:3; 1 Tim. 3:7)

Since it is unlikely that you can have extensive personal knowledge of all the emerging leaders you will work with, you must listen carefully to those who actually do know them. Peer respect will often reveal true character, while a candidate's existing leaders will be able to evaluate his potential ministry capacity.

Too often, however, assessments of this nature are based on hearsay, casual observation and insufficient information. To assess an emerging leader properly, decisions should be based on an integrated view of him drawn from the various perspectives held by the people who have directly led, worked with, and lived with him throughout his life.

6. Look for security in Christ.

The emerging leader must have a genuine relationship with Jesus Christ. This relationship will be the source of his character as well as his endurance during hard times. In addition, he will not compromise his integrity for the sake of being accepted by man, when he has first found deep acceptance in Christ.

7. Look for the willingness to serve and to make personal sacrifices for the Divine cause.

Timothy, by submitting to circumcision, demonstrated his willingness to suffer for the ministry:

> Paul wanted to take him along on the journey, so he circumcised him because of the Jews who lived in that area, for they all knew that his father was a Greek. (Acts 16:3)

Jesus emphasized the need for total commitment:

> The kingdom of heaven is like treasure hidden in a field. When a man found it, he hid it again, and then in his joy went and sold all he had and bought that field. Again, the kingdom of heaven is like a merchant looking for fine pearls. When he found one of great value, he went away and sold everything he had and bought it. (Matt. 13:44-45)

Consider the immediate response of those who Jesus chose to follow Him:

> "Come, follow me," Jesus said, "and I will make you fishers of men." At once they left their nets and followed him. When he had gone a little farther, he saw James son of Zebedee and his brother John in a boat, preparing their nets. Without delay he called them, and they left their father Zebedee in the boat with the hired men and followed him. (Mark 1:17-20)

People who are not willing to make the necessary sacrifice and who have their own list of terms and requirements are probably not the best choices.

Many ambitious people conceive of leadership as being the path to fame and fortune. In reality, Christian leadership is not about position, titles, power, authority, respect or privilege; it is an obligation to service and to self-sacrifice.

When Jesus' disciples sought the highest places in His kingdom, He taught them a profound lesson:

> They replied, "Let one of us sit at your right and the other at your left in your glory."... Jesus called them together and said, "You know that those who are regarded as rulers of the Gentiles lord it over them, and their high officials exercise authority over them. Not so with you. Instead, whoever wants to become great among you must be your servant, and whoever wants to be first must be slave of all. For even the Son of Man did not come to be served, but to serve, and to give his life as a ransom for many." (Mark 10:37, 42-45)

The Christian leader's attitude must be that he is an "unworthy servant" who has only done his duty:

> Suppose one of you had a servant plowing or looking after the sheep. Would he say to the servant when he comes in from the field, "Come along now and sit down to eat"? Would he not rather say, "Prepare my supper, get yourself ready and wait on me while I eat and drink; after that you may eat and drink"? Would he thank the servant because he did what he was told to do? So you also, when you have done everything you were told to do, should say, "We are unworthy servants; we have only done our duty." (Luke 17:7-10)

This is the spirit to look for in an emerging leader. Furthermore, if he is married, his spouse must also embrace this call to servanthood. She may not personally possess the same call to a specific leadership role, but if he is to succeed, she must stand united with him in her heart commitment to service and sacrifice. Leadership is hard. It comes with suffering, rejection and pain. There is often a high price to be paid to lead. The emerging leader and his spouse must embrace the cross that accompanies Christian leadership.

8.   Look for a genuine love for God's people.

Jesus requires that we express our love for Him in our love and commitment to His people.

> *The third time he said to him, "Simon son of John, do you love me?" Peter was hurt because Jesus asked him the third time, "Do you love me?" He said, "Lord, you know all things; you know that I love you." Jesus said, "Feed my sheep. (John 21:17)*

> *We love because he first loved us. If anyone says, "I love God," yet hates his brother, he is a liar. For anyone who does not love his brother, whom he has seen, cannot love God, whom he has not seen. And he has given us this command: Whoever loves God must also love his brother. (1 John 4:19-21)*

We must not, as many leaders do, use the people of God for our own promotion or to fulfill our own agendas. The foundation of our ministries must be a genuine love for the saints and a commitment to their highest good in God's purposes.

> *I have no one else like him, who takes a genuine interest in your welfare. For everyone looks out for his own interests, not those of Jesus Christ. (Phil. 2:20-21)*

This love will be tested profoundly and repeatedly over the years of ministry, so it must be present from the beginning in the heart of an emerging leader.

9. Look for responsibility.

The emerging leader should already be self-motivated and leading various initiatives. Since leadership involves being the one who moves ahead first, the leader must have the courage and the willingness to take risks, to take responsibility and to move ahead without always having to be told by someone to do so.

In addition, he must have a history of completing his work in spite of obstacles that arise. This can be determined by giving a group of people the responsibility to solve a problem that they are not used to dealing with. The person who grabs hold of the challenge and sees it through probably has the greatest leadership potential.

10. Look for accountability.

We should look for emerging leaders who are genuinely teachable, correctable and accountable. Someone may profess a deep allegiance to a leader, but this allegiance will only be tested when that leader attempts to correct the person or hold him accountable.

11. Look for the ability to learn from experience.

Leaders help people move to new and better places; the very nature of leadership involves going into the unknown. Consequently, the capacity to learn from experience – in particular to learn from one's mistakes – is a critical ability in a leader. Leaders are learners. The great leaders of the future are those who have the ability to learn from their experiences and who remain open to continuous learning.

12. Look for "big-picture" thinking.

One key characteristic that distinguishes potential leaders from potential managers is the ability to think across departmental issues, not just the ability to make a strong case for one department. When it comes to the allocation of resources, leaders have to prioritize between multiple, well-presented, legitimate causes. One can only do this against a "big-picture" vision that covers the entire scope of the church or organization. Good managers make good cases for their own departments, but often cannot see, or hear, the validity of parallel claims on resources.[30]

In addition, a "big-picture" thinker will be one who can create vision and share it with others. Consequently, a person who does not feel the excitement of challenge may not be the best choice.

Finally, an effective "big-picture" thinker will be a good listener and a good observer. He will not be so inward looking or self-absorbed that he cannot understand the organization's surrounding environment.

13. Look for "outside the box" thinking.

As well as being "big-picture" thinkers, effective leaders will also be able to generate creative responses to opportunities and problems.

Effective leaders challenge the status quo. They are always seeking God's best. They are continually seeking a better way to do something. Thus, a healthy leader will have a spirit of discontent that is not critical but constructive. The way to distinguish between criticism and constructive discontent is this: if a person says, "There's got to be a better way to do

---

[30] For more on this leader-manager distinction please see *Leaders & Managers: SpiritBuilt Leadership #5* by Malcolm Webber.

this," you can determine if there is leadership potential in him by asking, "What might that better way be?" If he has nothing to offer, then he is being critical, and not constructive. But if he has already thought of creative alternatives, then he has a constructive spirit of discontent.

At the same time, they must be practical in their thinking. Not everyone who has practical ideas will be a good leader, but effective leaders must be able to distinguish between practical ideas and impractical ones, or else they will end up wasting a great deal of the organization's time and resources.

14. Look for a desire to help others succeed.

A significant part of leadership involves working with others in teams, so it is vital that each leader has a heart to help his co-workers succeed.

> *Do nothing out of selfish ambition or vain conceit, but in humility consider others better than yourselves. Each of you should look not only to your own interests, but also to the interests of others. (Phil. 2:3-4)*

This attitude will reveal itself in ministry situations when the individual prays for and actively serves not only his own portion of the work, but also other areas of the ministry.

In addition, the emerging leader should be able to get along with others, possessing a certain measure of relational capacity.

15. Look for a realistic opinion of himself and others.

> *For by the grace given me I say to every one of you: Do not think of yourself more highly than you ought, but rather think of yourself with sober judgment, in accordance with the measure of faith God has given you. (Rom. 12:3)*

Those who demand perfection from themselves and others will not make good leaders. Effective leaders must be willing to accept reasonable mistakes. Perfectionists will be too afraid of mistakes to delegate responsibilities to others.

16. Ask yourself if you are the right one to help this emerging leader.

   Even when you clearly discern leadership potential in someone, you must still be sure that you can give the person the right environment he needs to grow and succeed. Paul, for example, recognized that Mark was better-placed under Barnabas' ministry than under his own (Acts 15:36-40).

17. Make necessary adjustments.

   It is quite likely that we will make mistakes in our choosing of emerging leaders and we should be prepared to make adjustments if we discover a "bad fit."

   In addition, we may also want to establish a probationary period to be sure we are working with the right ones.

18. Don't demand perfection.

   We cannot expect perfection or even a high degree of maturity in a young, emerging leader in the early stages of his development. But there must be the whole-hearted willingness to learn and to grow.

Individually or in your study group:

1. Please find biblical examples of the truth of each of the above principles.

2. Examine the way that you (or your church or organization) choose the emerging leaders you plan to work with. What specific improvements can you make to your process?

Part 4

Effective Leader Development Will Be:

Experiential

学以致用，百炼成钢

Learning serves the purpose of practice, while repeated struggles temper steel (strong life)

Leaders Learn By Doing

People learn by doing. Therefore, an effective leader development process integrates "classroom" instruction time with practical "in the field," "hands on" ministry. Leaders must be built "on the job." This involves two things.

First, the context for learning should be as similar as possible to the future leader's ultimate ministry environment. For example, if the future ministry of the worker will involve sleeping on a concrete floor and eating only one meal a day, then that should be his lifestyle while in training. Jesus built His emerging leaders in the same context in which they would ultimately be leading.

Second, the learning itself must involve doing. Jesus built His emerging leaders "on the job" where they dealt with real problems, explored real opportunities and faced real consequences.

The tragedy of the traditional approach to Christian leader development is that emerging leaders are removed from their normal context of life and ministry and placed in a protected, artificial environment (for years at a time), the nature of which will never be duplicated for the rest of their lives, and then they are taught things, much of which they will never use for the rest of their lives!

Leaders should be trained in the task, not away from it. The New Testament approach is along the lines of "on the job" training, not the withdrawal from society practiced by Western intellectual religious institutions. Jesus taught His disciples as He took them with Him. When He said, "Look on the fields; the harvest truly is great," He was in the midst of visible need. The harvest field was not something found on a map on the wall, but was rather portrayed in the needs of the sick and sinful multitudes that were surrounding them on every side. Jesus taught His disciples and then sent them out to preach and to heal the sick. When they failed, as in the case of the man with the epileptic son (Matt. 17:14-21) or Peter[31] (John 21:15-19), He gave them further instruction. He taught them as they ministered.

In Acts 19, Paul had a learning community in Ephesus where he taught for two years. But this was not classroom instruction only, since from this ministry "all the Jews and Greeks who lived in the province of Asia heard the word of the Lord" (Acts 19:10). As Paul taught, the believers and workers who were raised up under his ministry went out and accomplished this tremendous feat of evangelism. Thus, the New Testament does not preclude "ministry schools," but it does illustrate "on the job" training.

Jesus also spent some time instructing His disciples, but then He sent them out to do ministry. Sometimes He would be with them; other times, He would send them out by themselves.

From Jesus' ministry we see that learning must be integrated with doing. If it is all learning, it soon becomes boring and irrelevant. But when learning is integrated with doing, the doing gives application, context, relevance, reality, meaning, motivation and purpose to the learning. The people actually do learn!

One seminary leader noted that when the students first arrived at his seminary, they were on fire for God. However, after three or four years of training at the seminary, most of them had "died." His response was, "We need a better grade of student!" In reality, the students needed a better grade of seminary!

Years ago a young man said to the author, "I've spent the last seven years of my life and a huge sum of money in gaining an advanced religious education. Now I've finally graduated from university with a higher degree. In the eyes of the religious world I'm equipped, I'm qualified,

---

[31] Jesus used Peter's terrible experience of failure (when he denied Him three times) to teach him what he apparently could not have learned any other way!

I'm ready to go. But, in reality, I don't know where to go, what to do when I get there or how to do it!" This young man had graduated from quite a good institution, but he had a long way to go in being built as a leader. Like many leaders, he had some strong competencies in certain areas, but no overall context for those competencies, and huge lacks in some of the main areas of the Christian life!

Certainly there may be a few people who God has called in a special way to dedicate their lives to learning and to becoming expert in areas such as theology. However, most Christian leaders are not academics or scholars, but they work with people in the midst of the realities of life, and they need learning and doing to be integrated in their development.[32]

Here are two possible approaches to balancing learning and doing. In the first graphic, there are subsequent blocks of learning and doing. In the second, learning and doing are virtually simultaneous. The second approach is best, when there is engagement in both learning and doing at the same time. This is how Jesus built His disciples.

However, practical or security issues in many countries will dictate the need for the first approach, in which the emerging leaders are in a learning environment for a period of several weeks or months, after which they go out into the field with a ministry mentor for several weeks or months, before returning to the community for more learning.

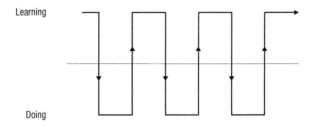

---

[32] As Ted Ward says, so much of our theological training sets forth tables full of food for giraffes, when God has called us to feed His sheep.

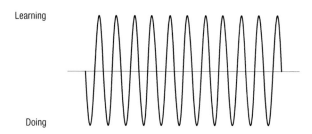

Once again, here is where the community helps, by providing opportunities for ministry and responsibilities – with real benefits and real consequences – in the very midst of the emerging leaders' learning.

People learn best by doing. Imagine a music student who arrives at violin school. He has never touched a violin but wants to learn to play. During his training at the school he is taught all about the violin: how it is made, its history, its use, how to read music, and the careers of great violinists. But he is never allowed to actually touch the instrument. After several years of this training, he passes the written exam and graduates. After graduation, in front of a large crowd of people, he is finally handed a violin. Expectations are high, since his grades were very good. He is asked to play this violin for everyone. But will he be able to?

Sadly, this story is an accurate metaphor for much Christian ministerial training that occurs today.

An old Chinese proverb says, "Tell me and I'll forget. Show me and I may remember. Involve me and I'll understand." In other words, people learn by doing.

Paul gave his emerging leaders practical responsibilities and experiences. For example:

- When he wanted to raise up Timothy he took him with him (Acts 16:1-3).
- Silas accompanied Paul not only in the classroom but also in

the prison (Acts 16:22-24)!

- Paul left Silas and Timothy in Berea to minister by themselves (Acts 17:14-15).
- Paul left Titus in Crete to establish the new churches (Tit. 1:5).
- Timothy was considered Paul's "fellow-worker" in the gospel (Rom. 16:21; Phil. 2:22; 1 Thess. 3:2; 1 Cor. 16:10). He ministered as he learned.
- Paul trusted Timothy with several difficult assignments in churches: Thessalonica (1 Thess. 3:1-6), Corinth (1 Cor. 4:16-17; 16:10-11), Philippi (Phil. 2:19-24), and Ephesus (1 Tim. 1:3).

This was how Paul built leaders – he built them "on the job," integrating learning and doing.

Classroom instruction, by itself, is not sufficient to build new leaders. Leader development is much bigger than education or formal training. There is a part for formal instruction to play in the process, but it is not enough by itself. God uses all the processes of life in the extremely complicated course of building a leader.

In view of the profound limitations of a classroom environment, it is useful to identify exactly what can be accomplished well in a formal classroom.

WHAT CAN BE ACCOMPLISHED IN THE CLASSROOM?

Most aspects of leadership cannot be learned in the classroom. They are the outcomes of years of diverse experiences and relationships coupled with the gifts of the leader. For example, what leaders often call "intuition" in making effective decisions is in reality a decision-making capacity based on years of trial-and-error experiences in similar situations – or, what one could call "spiritual wisdom."

However, there are certain things that can profitably be addressed in a formal classroom or training setting as long as they take place within the broader context of the experiences of life and ministry.

1. For Christian leaders, formal training must include deep and systematic teaching of the Word of God.

   All Scripture is God-breathed and is useful for teaching, rebuking, correcting and training in righteousness, so that the man of God may be thoroughly equipped for every good work. (2 Tim. 3:16-17)

2. Simple skill building. In many organizations, the development of skills on-the-job is a largely haphazard process, in that the learning usually occurs by chance. Thus, it is likely that certain leadership skills will never be learned or will be developed only partially. Training can formalize this process and ensure the emerging leader receives correct and adequate exposure to particular necessary skills.

   There are two kinds of skills that need to be developed in leaders:

   a. Ministry skills. This is the day-to-day specialized knowledge needed to lead in a particular organizational context; for example, prayer, deliverance, healing, music, leading worship, counseling, communication, preaching the gospel, sharing one's personal testimony, etc.

b. People skills. These interpersonal skills, such as developing teams, managing change, communication, listening, accountability, giving and receiving correction, cross-cultural skills, conflict management, delegation, etc., are always necessary, but frequently neglected!

3. Conceptual abilities or how to think.

a. Strategic skills. As leaders grow in responsibility, they must make the profound strategic transition from doing things well to seeing that those things are done well. Thus, strategic skills, such as interpreting the environment, systems thinking, assessing follower needs, strategic envisioning and planning, etc., are necessary, especially at higher levels in the organization.

b. Big picture thinking. Effective leaders often have a strong ability to think conceptually – to see the big picture. This plays a vital role in their ability to set direction because the ability to think strategically involves comprehending the current and future environments. Visionary leaders can think clearly over relatively long spans of time, seeing how complicated chains of events are related, and developing practical strategies for attaining long-range goals. Formal training can encourage the leader to think conceptually about the issues facing his organization by giving him conceptual frameworks and models to use in interpreting information. The rest of his conceptual development will then come through his relationship with God, his experiences, and his interactions with others who are also working through "big picture" issues.

Jesus shared many "big picture" conceptual frameworks with His disciples (e.g., Matt. 20:25-28) as did Paul (e.g., 1 Cor. 12).

c. Clarity regarding the role of the leader. Another aspect of conceptual ability is the leader's ability to understand the leadership role itself – to understand what leadership is and the differences between a leader and a manager, and to know how to be and act like a leader. These things are often learned through observing successful and unsuccessful leaders in various contexts. Additionally, formal training can expose emerging leaders to a diversity of leadership examples and provide simple models to help define leadership. Thus, training helps build the awareness that will greatly enhance and give meaning to the experiences of life and ministry.

It is not sufficient merely to teach an emerging leader about these conceptual abilities. There is still the responsibility on the part of both the leader and his community to create the subsequent leadership experiences that will make the conceptual understandings an integral and lasting part of the leader's thinking.

4. Personal reflection exercises.

Emerging leaders need time to consolidate learning. So we must provide some time for reflection and analysis. Unfortunately, much experience, both positive and negative, is wasted because leaders aren't allowed – or forced – to stop and make sense of what just happened or to digest what they just learned. Without sufficient reflection, people tend to repeat their mistakes. Reflection is hard to do in the field.

a. Through training and personal exercises, the leader can reflect upon his relationships with God and his community that lie at the heart of his leadership. He can also examine his own character. Ideally, these reflective exercises should begin early in a leader's life, and occur regularly.

    b. Reflective exercises can also stimulate personal growth by heightening a person's awareness of his own personality and cultural predispositions, as well as his competency strengths and weaknesses.

    c. Purpose exercises can help the emerging leader to clarify his own calling from God. The more accurately he can do this, the more effective he will be.

Personal reflection can be done in a variety of contexts: individually, in pairs with a peer or with an advisor, mentor or coach, or in a small group.

5. Intensive feedback. It is profitable for the leader to receive candid feedback from others regarding the present condition of his leadership with regard to the prior four areas. For example, one might ask, "How are my communication skills and in what areas do I need improvement?" This will help him to fully understand his strengths and weaknesses, and to define a plan for future development. This feedback will be especially effective when it occurs in the context of the intense relationships of daily life within the learning community.

Individually or in your study group:

1. Please find Old Testament examples of "on the job" leader development.

2. From the ministry of Paul – from Acts and from his epistles – please find examples of how he built leaders "on the job."

Challenging Assignments Stretch and Mature the Emerging Leader

Over the last century, there has been a vast amount of academic research in the social sciences concerning many aspects of leadership. However, there has not been a great deal of research concerning how leaders are built – due to the complex nature of this subject. But according to the research that has been done, the two things that contribute the most to the formation of emerging leaders are:

1. Leaders they have known and served – mentors and role models with whom they have had direct personal contact.

2. Challenging assignments they were given.

Mark 3:14-15 summarizes these two aspects of Jesus' primary method of building leaders: His own personal relationship with them and challenging assignments.

> *He appointed twelve – designating them apostles – that they might be with him and that he might send them out to preach and to have authority to drive out demons. (Mark 3:14-15)*

Therefore, as we have already observed, our processes of leader development must involve significant personal time with leaders and mentors, as well as exposure to many leaders (both good and bad). Now we will deal with the role of challenging assignments.

As the following graphic shows, a "challenging assignment" is one that is a little bit above the emerging leader's present perceived capacity.[33] They should not be too far above or else he will fail and be discouraged and give up. But the assignment should not be below or equal to his capacity. Thus, the assignment will *stretch* him; since it is above his present capacity, he will be forced to look to God for help, and to learn and grow, and to move outside of his normal actions and reactions. As he succeeds in these stretching assignments, he should be given progressively harder ones. This series of successive victories will build his character and his faith in God as well as teach him new capacities.[34]

Give Stretching Assignments!

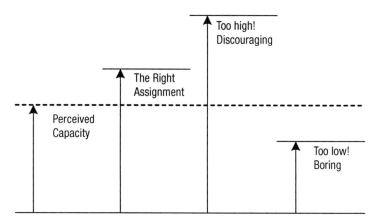

A challenging assignment is like a rubber band:

---

[33] But do not give him responsibilities beyond his *character* (1 Tim. 3:6, 10; 5:22-25)! In addition, a challenging assignment does not necessarily have to involve a *positional promotion*. In fact, some assignments are more challenging without a positional promotion!

[34] Vygotsky, a Russian educational philosopher, talked about the Zone of Proximal Development (ZPD). It is the difference between where learners are and where their teachers expect them to be at any given moment. If the ZPD is too large (expectations are too high) then the learner becomes frustrated and discouraged. If the ZPD is too small (expectations are too low) then the learner is bored and loses interest. When the ZPD is optimal, the learner is stretched, but not beyond his or her limit.

- Once stretched, it never returns to its original shape.
- If stretched too far, it will break.
- If released at the wrong time, it will hurt everyone involved.

Challenging assignments develop all the important areas of a leader's life and ministry and build the following:

- faith in God
- confidence
- clear knowledge of God's purpose
- acceptance of responsibility
- spiritual discernment
- increased biblical insight
- growth in spiritual warfare
- strengthened prayer life
- endurance
- persistence
- practical knowledge
- coping with ambiguity
- ability to analyze a situation and identify what is important
- innovative problem-solving methods
- appreciation of the difficulties of working with people
- knowledge of one's own limits and blind spots
- appreciation of one's need for others
- ability to recognize and seize opportunities
- skill in managing relationships
- understanding of how much leadership matters, and how difficult the role can be

In addition, the leader must know when to leave the person alone, trusting him to take full responsibility for the assignment. Jesus did this and He did not wait until His disciples were perfect. In Mark 16, Jesus gave His disciples an extraordinary assignment (the Great Commission) immediately after they had failed three times (vv. 8, 11, 13-14)![35] And then He

---

[35] Like Jesus, many times the experienced leader will believe in the emerging leader more than he does himself!

left! Two thousand years later, almost 700 million believers around the world demonstrate the wisdom of Jesus' strategy: it worked! Certainly, Jesus' disciples made some errors along the way, but in the long term this strategy worked!

Emerging leaders will carry these experiences with them throughout their later ministries. Thus, it is important that stretching assignments be given to them early in their lives – to have maximum effect on their lives and ministries. Don't wait until they're perfect!

The Bible is replete with challenging assignments:

> *By this time it was late in the day, so his disciples came to him. "This is a remote place," they said, "and it's already very late. Send the people away so they can go to the surrounding countryside and villages and buy themselves something to eat." But he answered, "You give them something to eat."... (Mark 6:35-37)*

> *When Jesus looked up and saw a great crowd coming toward him, he said to Philip, "Where shall we buy bread for these people to eat?" He asked this only to test him, for he already had in mind what he was going to do. (John 6:5-6)*

> *Then Jesus came to them and said, "All authority in heaven and on earth has been given to me. Therefore go and make disciples of all nations, baptizing them in the name of the Father and of the Son and of the Holy Spirit, and teaching them to obey everything I have commanded you. And surely I am with you always, to the very end of the age." (Matt. 28:18-20)*

> *Some time later God tested Abraham. He said to him, "Abraham!" "Here I am," he replied. Then God said, "Take your son, your only son, Isaac, whom you love, and go to the region of Moriah. Sacrifice him there as a burnt offering on one of the mountains I will tell you about." (Gen. 22:1-2; cf. Heb. 11:17-19)*

But so that we may not offend them, go to the lake and throw out your line. Take the first fish you catch; open its mouth and you will find a four-drachma coin. Take it and give it to them for my tax and yours. (Matt. 17:27)

These twelve Jesus sent out with the following instructions: "Do not go among the Gentiles or enter any town of the Samaritans. Go rather to the lost sheep of Israel. As you go, preach this message: 'The kingdom of heaven is near.' Heal the sick, raise the dead, cleanse those who have leprosy, drive out demons. Freely you have received, freely give. Do not take along any gold or silver or copper in your belts; take no bag for the journey, or extra tunic, or sandals or a staff; for the worker is worth his keep. (Matt. 10:5-10; see also Luke 9:1-6; 10:1-12; 22:8-13; Matt. 3:13-15; 14:29; 21:2; Luke 1:26-38; Acts 17:14-15; 1 Thess. 3:2; John 6:53; 13:8; 21:6, 17; Gen. 15:5; 2 Kings 2; Esther 4:14)

This is how people grow – when they are entrusted with challenging assignments.

"CHALLENGING ASSIGNMENTS" AND "TASKS"

Leaders who build leaders must balance current and legitimate organizational needs with their emerging leaders' needs for growth.

A leader who puts the needs of the organization first will likely not be good at giving "challenging assignments," but, instead, will play it safe and assign his emerging leaders "tasks" that lie well within their capacities to accomplish successfully.

There is some degree of organizational risk involved in giving challenging assignments. Of course, every organization has certain critical tasks that should be assigned conservatively. However, there are also many opportunities for emerging leaders' growth.

If your priority is building people then you will design challenging assignments for them; if your priority is to take care of organizational needs, then you will assign tasks.

Somehow, these two priorities must be balanced. Tasks benefit the organization; challenging assignments benefit the emerging leaders. Tasks focus on the present; challenging assignments focus on the future. Tasks serve the situation; challenging assignments serve the emerging leaders.

Leaders who build leaders design for them appropriate challenging assignments.

It is through fire and challenge that strong men and women of God are built!

> The best training for a soldier of Christ is not merely a theological college. They always seem to turn out sausages of varying lengths, tied at each end, without the glorious freedom a Christian ought to abound and rejoice in.
>
> You see, when in hand-to-hand conflict with the world and the devil, neat little biblical confectionery is like shooting lions with a pea-shooter: one needs a man who will let himself go and deliver blows right and left as hard as he can hit, trusting in the Holy Ghost.
>
> It's experience, not preaching that hurts the devil and confounds the world. The training is not that of the schools but of the market: it's the hot, free heart and not the balanced head that knocks the devil out. Nothing but forked-lightning Christians will count.
>
> A lost reputation is the best degree for Christ's service. It is not so much the degree of arts that is needed, but that of hearts, loyal and true, that love not their lives to the death: large and loving hearts which seek to save the lost multitudes, rather than guard the ninety-nine well-fed sheep in the British pen. (C.T. Studd)

If we want to build tough, visionary leaders who will change their worlds, we must give them challenging assignments.

Individually or in your study group:

1. Please find biblical examples of emerging leaders being given stretching assignments.

2. Please think of some challenging assignments God (or a leader in your life) has given you.

Leaders Are Built Through Fire

Leaders are built through fire – like steel is made hard in the fire, like gold is purified in the furnace, like carbon is formed under pressure into diamonds.[36]

Pressure reveals the impurities in one's life so they can be dealt with. It is far better to put the emerging leader under pressure before he is given significant responsibility and authority than to wait until the time when failure under pressure will destroy both the leader and those with him. Therefore, the development process can intentionally put the participants under a certain amount of pressure to squeeze heart contaminations to the surface so they can be revealed, confronted and removed.

Of course, this is how God deals with all of us. He has always used suffering as a vital part of the Christian life.

> *For it has been granted to you on behalf of Christ not only to believe on him, but also to suffer for him, (Phil. 1:29)*
>
> *If we suffer, we shall also reign with him... (2 Tim. 2:12, KJV)*
>
> *...now for a little while you may have had to suffer grief in all kinds[37] of trials. These have come so that your faith...may be proved genuine and may result in praise, glory and honor when Jesus Christ is revealed. (1 Pet. 1:6-7)*
>
> *...those who suffer according to God's will should commit themselves to their faithful Creator and continue to do good. (1 Pet. 4:19)*

---

[36] Significantly, the formation of diamonds from carbon requires three things: (1) *extreme pressures,* 100 miles or more deep under the earth's surface, (2) *high temperatures,* 2000 °F or more, and (3) *time,* diamonds are formed very slowly.
[37] Not only persecution, but "all kinds" of suffering.

Dear friends, do not be surprised at the painful trial you are suffering, as though something strange were happening to you. But rejoice that you participate in the sufferings of Christ, so that you may be overjoyed when his glory is revealed. (1 Pet. 4:12-13)

In particular, suffering is a vital part of *leadership*. Godly leaders know that sufferings can build spiritual maturity, brokenness and genuine faith in God; thus, they do not shy away from the cross in their lives.

Paul's cry was:

I want to know Christ and the power of his resurrection and the fellowship of sharing in his sufferings, becoming like him in his death, and so, somehow, to attain to the resurrection from the dead. (Phil. 3:10-11)

Look closely: Paul said, "I want to know…the fellowship of sharing in His sufferings." Paul actually desired to suffer with Jesus! This was not because he enjoyed pain in some perverse way, but because he knew that the greatest place of union with God is found in the dark shadows of rejection and suffering. Paul knew that we only find God's deep presence when we have been united with Him in His sufferings and death. Paul knew that the cross precedes the crown, darkness precedes glory, brokenness precedes true victory, death precedes true life.

Accordingly, Jesus showed the way of suffering to the leaders He was building. He personally demonstrated sufferings to them:

- The sufferings of rejection as He was scorned and rejected by the religious leaders.

  He was despised and rejected by men, a man of sorrows, and familiar with suffering. Like one from whom men hide their faces he was despised, and we esteemed him not. (Is. 53:3)

- The suffering of His human struggle with obedience to God.

...My Father, if it is possible, may this cup be taken from me. Yet not as I will, but as you will. (Matt. 26:39)

In bringing many sons to glory, it was fitting that God, for whom and through whom everything exists, should make the author of their salvation perfect through suffering. (Heb. 2:10)

Although he was a son, he learned obedience from what he suffered (Heb. 5:8)

- The suffering of the cross as He was lifted up from the ground and hung before them.

But I, when I am lifted up from the earth, will draw all men to myself. (John 12:32)

Paul also demonstrated the cross before the people he raised up as leaders:

You, however, know all about my teaching, my way of life, my purpose, faith, patience, love, endurance, persecutions, sufferings – what kinds of things happened to me in Antioch, Iconium and Lystra, the persecutions I endured. Yet the Lord rescued me from all of them. (2 Tim. 3:10-11)

Today, many Christian leaders are offered the temptation of power without suffering. In fact, in the Western world we devise entire theologies to justify our lack of suffering and our love of pleasure. "If you have enough faith you will never suffer." "If you just believe and confess it, God will deliver you from adversity and suffering of every kind." However, when Peter tried to talk Jesus into such a theology, he was sternly rebuked:

Get behind me, Satan! You are a stumbling block to me; you do not have in mind the things of God, but the things of men. (Matt. 16:23)

Jesus refused a "cross-less" leadership. He knew there is no true authority without sacrifice. There is no true spiritual maturity without suffering. There is no true leadership without the cross.

If anyone would come after me, he must deny himself and take up his cross and follow me. For whoever wants to save his life will lose it, but whoever loses his life for me will find it. (Matt. 16:24-25)

This was the kind of leadership Jesus taught His disciples: a leadership born of brokenness, produced in pain, forged in the fire of suffering. He taught this and modeled it to them.

Many biblical leaders such as Joseph, Moses, David and Paul were built this way.

You, however, know all about my teaching, my way of life, my purpose, faith, patience, love, endurance, persecutions, sufferings – what kinds of things happened to me in Antioch, Iconium and Lystra, the persecutions I endured. Yet the Lord rescued me from all of them. In fact, everyone who wants to live a godly life in Christ Jesus will be persecuted, (2 Tim. 3:10-12)

Praise be to the God and Father of our Lord Jesus Christ, the Father of compassion and the God of all comfort, who comforts us in all our troubles, so that we can comfort those in any trouble with the comfort we ourselves have received from God. For just as the sufferings of Christ flow over into our lives, so also through Christ our comfort overflows. (2 Cor. 1:3-5)

We do not want you to be uninformed, brothers, about the hardships we suffered in the province of Asia. We were under great pressure, far beyond our ability to endure, so that we despaired even of life. Indeed, in our hearts we felt the sentence of death. But this happened that we might not rely on ourselves but on God, who raises the dead. He has delivered us from such a deadly peril, and he will deliver us. On him we have set our hope that he will continue to deliver us, as you help us by your prayers. Then many will give thanks on our behalf for the gracious favor granted us in answer to the prayers of many. (2 Cor. 1:8-11; see also 4:7-12; 11:21-29;)

These are the ways of God: healthy leaders are built – and lead – in the fires of suffering.

Then the mother of Zebedee's sons came to Jesus with her sons and, kneeling down, asked a favor of him. "What is it you want?" he asked. She said, "Grant that one of these two sons of mine may sit at your right and the other at your left in your kingdom." "You don't know what you are asking," Jesus said to them. "Can you drink the cup I am going to drink?"... (Matt. 20:20-22)

Consider it pure joy, my brothers, whenever you face trials of many kinds, because you know that the testing of your faith develops perseverance. Perseverance must finish its work so that you may be mature and complete, not lacking anything. (Jam. 1:2-4; cf. Ps. 119:71)

... we also rejoice in our sufferings, because we know that suffering produces perseverance; perseverance, character; and character... (Rom. 5:3-4)

As Abigail Adams wrote to her son John Quincy:

These are the times in which a genius would wish to live. It is not in the still calm of life, or the repose of a pacific station, that great characters are formed. The habits of a vigorous mind are formed in contending with difficulties. Great necessities call out great virtues. When a mind is raised, and animated by scenes that engage the heart, then those qualities which would otherwise lay dormant, wake into life and form the character of the hero and the statesman.

Or, in the words of Helen Keller:

Character cannot be developed in ease and quiet. Only through experiences of trial and suffering can the soul be strengthened, vision cleared, ambition inspired, and success achieved.

PRACTICAL IMPLICATIONS FOR BUILDERS

Jesus used pressure to refine the character of His disciples. Mark 6 gives an example:

> *When evening came, the boat was in the middle of the lake, and he was alone on land. He saw the disciples straining at the oars, because the wind was against them. About the fourth watch of the night he went out to them, walking on the lake. (Mark 6:47-48)*

Jesus allowed His disciples to struggle against the wind for nine hours – from "evening" (about 6 PM) to the "fourth watch" (about 3 AM)! He could have stopped the storm at any time, but He sat and watched them go through it.

Jesus used pressure to mould His disciples both actively (creating situations of pressure) and passively (taking advantage of circumstances). An effective leader development process will do the same.

While the learning community itself should be a relational haven of peace and blessing, at the same time it should not be exempted from the rigors of having to trust God for the practical necessities of life and ministry. For example, the builder should not bear all the financial responsibility for any learning community by himself, but should allow the emerging leaders to help him carry the load of trusting God for daily financial provision. Accordingly, the disciples stood with Jesus in faith for provision. He didn't shelter them (e.g., Matt. 17:27; Mark 6:35-37).

In addition, we should not shield emerging leaders from unpleasant or difficult circumstances, such as:

141

- personal or family traumas
- intense spiritual warfare
- persecution for their faith
- leadership rejection
- career setbacks involving demotions and missed promotions
- relational conflicts
- leadership mistakes, in which bad judgment and poor decisions lead to failure
- having to deal with problem subordinates (one of the most dreaded of all leadership responsibilities)

Allowing them to go through hardship will teach emerging leaders many things, such as:

- reliance on God
- deeper submission to God's will
- responding with grace and forgiveness, instead of bitterness and anger
- sensitivity to others
- coping with personal rejection
- coping with events beyond one's own control
- personal limits
- integrating family responsibilities and ministry responsibilities
- endurance

Naturally, we cannot expect to deal with every issue or problem in the emerging leader's life during the training period. However, during this time the young leader will become better prepared to deal with his own struggles later on:

1. He will learn how to establish relational webs of nurture, support and accountability that he will hopefully maintain for the rest of his life.

2. He will learn how to open his heart and life to others around him, becoming vulnerable and honest.

3. He will learn how to receive help from others.

There are several cautions we must observe as we introduce pressure into the lives of emerging leaders:

1. It is not true that "the more we make them suffer, the more they will grow." God allows suffering in our lives, but He does so wisely. We should not just callously or arbitrarily throw people into the fire, thinking this will automatically improve them.

   We should be intentional and careful about exposing emerging leaders to various forms of pressure. A boxer said to his manager, "I want to fight the champ." The manager said, "No, you're not ready for the champ." "But I want to fight him. I'm ready. Why can't I fight him?" "Because," said the manager, "you've only so many fights in you, and it's my job to pick the right ones." In the same way, we need to protect our emerging leaders by carefully designing what they experience.

2. It is not the suffering itself that purifies us – it is how we respond to the suffering that counts. Suffering can go both ways – it can hurt us or help us (Matt. 21:44). Sadly, the reality is that most people are hurt through their suffering.

3. It should not be a constant fire. God allows us to suffer for "a little while" (1 Pet. 1:6; 5:10); this suffering is not continuous, but periodic, from time to time.

4. It should not be to the extent that it destroys them. God does not allow us to be tested beyond what we can bear (1 Cor. 10:13).

5. In the midst of suffering and pressure, emerging leaders need comfort. When God allows suffering, He often does not give deliverance from it, but comfort in it (2 Cor. 1:3-5). God

allows us to go through the fire, but He does not leave us alone in the fire (Dan. 3:25). Thus, before we introduce pressure, we must ensure that a supportive community has first been built around the emerging leaders.

Here are some specific ways in which pressure can be created to build character in emerging leaders:

- Difficult assignments that are beyond their ability. Jesus left his disciples to deal with the demonized boy when it was beyond their capacity (Matt. 17:16). A new situation where mistakes in action and judgment may become obvious to others demands genuine humility and moral courage.
- Giving them the opportunity to give up (cf. John 6:67).
- Confusing assignments that are unclear or ambiguous.
- Multiple assignments of different kinds at the same time.
- Simply being required to work in teams; this is very hard for some people.
- "Interesting" team combinations. (Do not put all the "people-people" together in the same teams.)
- Changing teams regularly.
- Deadlines.
- Circumstantial accidents.
- Specific assignments that create possible rejection, etc.
- Humbling service.
- Limited resources.
- Challenging ministry responsibilities.
- Balancing relationships and tasks.
- Spontaneous assignments.

As we prayerfully and carefully introduce pressure into our leader development design, we will give our emerging leaders the opportunity to more deeply embrace the cross and the resurrection life that follows.

Individually or in your study group:

1. Please find biblical examples of different kinds of pressure that God used in the forming of emerging leaders in both testaments.

2. From your own experience, please think of examples of each of the following kinds of suffering. Describe what happened, how you reacted, and how it affected you in the long-term:

   a. Personal or family traumas.
   b. Intense spiritual warfare.
   c. Persecution for the faith.
   d. Leadership rejection.
   e. Demotions.
   f. Relational conflicts.
   g. Leadership mistakes, in which bad judgment and poor decisions led to failure.
   h. Having to deal with problem subordinates.

Part 5

Effective Leader Development Will Be:

Instructional

学习真理，活出生命

To study the Truth, and to live out its reality

The Word of God Is the Foundation and the Means for Building Healthy Leaders

The teaching of the Word of God was central in Jesus' method of building leaders.

Jesus was a teacher. Of course, His teaching was not only by words; He also demonstrated the truths He taught to His disciples. His personal example illustrated and authenticated what He taught. Moreover, He led His disciples into their own personal experiences of the truth. Yet, at the heart of it all – and surrounding it all – was His teaching of the Word of God.

The teaching of the Word was central in Jesus' ministry. Many times in the gospels we read that Jesus "began to teach...." He taught in public, He taught in large groups, He taught in small groups, He taught individuals privately, He taught the lost, He taught His followers, He taught His emerging leaders. The Word of God was central in His life, His ministry and His method.

Then, before He returned to heaven, Jesus told His leaders to go and do the same thing: "go and make disciples of all nations... teaching them to obey everything I have commanded you" (Matt. 28:19-20). Thus, throughout the book of Acts, the Word of God was central in the life of the early church. They won the lost by teaching the Word, they planted churches by teaching the Word, they built those churches by teaching the Word, they raised up leaders through teaching the Word, and they spent a lot of time and energy in keeping the church's teaching free from imbalance and corruption. The Word of God was central.

Neither Jesus nor the early church leaders were satisfied with sharing brief sermonettes on "felt-needs" once a week on Sunday mornings. They spent hours, days, weeks, months, even years patiently and passionately teaching the Word of God. Moreover, they never shrank back from teaching the Word even when they were rejected for it (John 6:59-68).

This was how Jesus and the early church raised up strong leaders: through the teaching of the strong Word of God. Jesus and the apostles were utterly committed to the truth and they raised up leaders with the same passion.

It is not hard to prove that the Word of God is not so central in our churches today. When was the last time you heard a serious exposition of one of Paul's letters in church on Sunday morning? Even in our seminaries and Bible schools we require our students to spend more time studying the words of men than the simple Word of God.

We have become more pragmatic than passionate; more concerned for temporal expediency than for eternity; more interested in image-management than with the true image of Jesus being formed in His people. We are considerably better managers than we are martyrs. We are more engaged with "effectiveness" (aka numbers – of people and dollars) than with idealism.

Many of the New Testament epistles were written to bring doctrinal and practical correction to the local churches. Today we promote seminars to help people be better leaders – regardless of what they believe and teach. We just want them to be "better leaders"! Outward appearance has become all important to us; too often we neglect the inner substance.

We need to remember that the church is called to be "the pillar and foundation of the truth" (1 Tim. 3:15), and that God's leaders are called both to confirm (by preaching the truth) and defend (by opposing the errors) the gospel (Phil. 1:7).

At the end of Jesus' ministry, He could only claim a handful of followers. Yet He was able to say, "I have finished the work which You have given Me to do" (John 17:4, NKJV).

In his last letter before he was executed, Paul wrote, "You know that everyone in the province of Asia has deserted me" (2 Tim. 1:15). Yet, he too was able to say, "I have fought the good fight, I have finished the race, I have kept the faith" (2 Tim. 4:7).

Whether we ever accomplish anything that the world marvels at is irrelevant. Whether we are ever respected or even accepted by the world's elite is meaningless. What counts – what alone counts – is whether we fight the good fight, whether we confirm and defend the truth, whether we keep the faith.

Leaders who put "effectiveness" first and truth second may achieve greatness in this life, but, in God's eyes, their lives and ministries are trivial. The example we set before the next generation of emerging leaders must be one of men and women who loved, proclaimed, fought for, and, if necessary, died for the truth of the Word of God.

PRACTICAL IMPLICATIONS FOR BUILDERS

First, there must be a balance of the teaching of the Word of God and personal relationship with the leader.

Paul emphasized teaching:

> You, however, know all about my teaching... (2 Tim. 3:10-11; see also Col. 1:6, 28; 1 Tim. 4:6; Tit. 1:9)

He also emphasized relationship:

> You, however, know all about...my way of life, my purpose, faith, patience, love, endurance, persecutions, sufferings... (2 Tim. 3:10-11)

The sharing of teaching must be integrated with the sharing of life.

But as for you, continue in what you have learned and have become convinced of, because you know those from whom you learned it, and how from infancy you have known the holy Scriptures, which are able to make you wise for salvation through faith in Christ Jesus. (2 Tim. 3:14-15; cf. 1 Cor. 4:17)

Second, as the next principle will demonstrate, there must be engagement with the teaching. The emerging leaders need to be given practical assignments of some kind to teach them to apply the Word. They must learn and do.

Without practical application, endless teaching will become quite harmful, resulting in pride and useless knowledge (1 Cor. 8:1).

Teaching is not necessarily learning. Teaching involves what you *know*; learning involves what you actually *do*. Nothing has been effectively taught until the behavior has changed.

All Scripture is God-breathed and is useful for teaching, rebuking, correcting and training in righteousness, so that the man of God may be thoroughly equipped for every good work. (2 Tim. 3:16-17)

Third, the best form of teaching will often be an interactive dialogue between participant and teacher – not merely an endless monologue to which the student passively listens. Lecturing is not often the best way for learning to occur. Listening is not learning. Learning requires activity.

This was how Jesus taught in the gospels: He interacted with His emerging leaders, asking them questions (e.g., Matt. 16:13-19).

Fourth, we must teach the Word and not merely about the Word. In the Word of God, there is power to change lives and build leaders. In practical terms, this means we should spend more time in the Bible than in books written about the Bible.

The following is a wonderful example of the power of the Word of God:

> When Billy Graham was called to the ministry he went to Florida Bible Institute for his training. He recalls that the school was a nurturing place that offered a variety of opportunities to test his preaching skills – from street corners and rural churches to his favorite audience at "Tin Can Trailer Park." Florida Bible Institute had only one real curriculum: the Bible. The greatest strength of this curriculum for Graham was the way it encouraged him to immerse himself in the content of the Bible. Most academic settings, even many religious ones, force students to keep the biblical message at arm's length. At Florida Bible Institute, Graham soaked himself in Scripture: reading Scripture, studying Scripture, pondering Scripture, preaching Scripture, applying Scripture. During those years, "Bible" flowed from every pore of his body. He thought Bible, he spoke Bible, he prayed Bible. Graham also learned another lesson during his early years of proclaiming the gospel. In 1955 at Cambridge University, Graham tried for three nights to make his preaching academic and erudite, but his efforts had no effect. Finally, realizing that his gift was not to present the intellectual side of faith, he abandoned his prepared texts and in utter simplicity preached the gospel message of our alienation from God because of sin and our reconciliation to God through the cross of Christ. The results were astonishing: hundreds of sophisticated students responded to this clear proclamation of the gospel. It was a lesson in clarity and simplicity that he never forgot.
> (From *Streams of Living Water* by Richard Foster)

Fifth, our teaching should be practical and relevant. One of the central characteristics of Greek culture, which is the foundation of modern Western culture, is the thirst for knowledge for its own sake.

> *All the Athenians and the foreigners who lived there* [at the Areopagus or Mars' hill] *spent their time doing nothing but talking about and listening to the latest ideas. (Acts 17:21)*

Jews demand miraculous signs and Greeks look for wisdom, but we preach Christ crucified: a stumbling block to Jews and foolishness to Gentiles, (1 Cor. 1:22-23)

The following is taken from *A Christian Critique of the University* by Charles Habib Malik.[38]

> The university is one of the greatest institutions of Western civilization... [being] more distinctive of Western civilization than of any other.
>
> The original model of this institution is the Brotherhood of Pythagoras and the Academy of Plato. All universities trace their ultimate origin to these two ancient Greek intellectual communities...
>
> The reason the universities of the world are Greek in ultimate origin stems from the nature of knowledge and the nature of the genius of the Greeks. The Greeks, more than any other people, displayed an irrepressible and unbounded passion for the exercise of reason and an incredible curiosity to investigate and know everything; and the university is nothing if it is not the home of free inquiry and unfettered curiosity...

According to Malik, more than by anything else, Western civilization is *defined* by total fearlessness of and openness to new knowledge – an insatiable thirst to know everything that can be known, a belief that everything that *can* be known *should* be known. This is knowledge for its own sake – whether or not it is of any practical significance. This explains why Western societies are content to spend billions of dollars in scientific research on outer space, when multitudes of people still live in poverty

---

[38] Dr. Malik (1906-87) was a brilliant scholar, earning his Ph.D. at Harvard and receiving over 50 honorary doctorates from American, Canadian and European universities. He served as Lebanese ambassador to the United States and as President of the General Assembly of the United Nations, among other appointments.

on our own planet. This is why some Christian theologians spend their lives studying nuances of obscure doctrines when hundreds of entire people groups still do not have a single church.

> *... There will be terrible times in the last days. People will be... always learning but never able to acknowledge the truth. (2 Tim. 3:1-7)*

This is knowledge for its own sake and Western civilization inherited this passion from the Greeks. Moreover, this disposition is instilled in our traditional Christian learning institutions.

A friend was invited to speak at a seminary function in the Central African Republic. His assigned topic related to "theological education." As he spoke, he noticed that his translator was taking a long time to translate the term "theological education." When asked how he was translating this idea, the translator responded, "I'm saying, 'A place where little boys go to get big heads.'"

The following are comments from rural house church leaders in Asia:

- In the past, developing competencies was our emphasis. As a result, we made students who were full of knowledge and proud but who couldn't solve practical problems in real life.
- In the last 10 years, our leadership training has become more and more Western, following Western models of seminaries and Bible schools. As a result, the quality of our newly raised leaders has declined.
- The Western approaches to training have not been successful. Our young people finish the school with big heads but little hearts. They have much new knowledge but their character is weak.
- Our young people who have gone through seminary training have become proud and somewhat alienated from the older generation. They have more knowledge now – they've had training that the older generation has never had. As a result they've become alienated; the social order has been damaged.

- Much of the Western theology that has come to our country is "junk theology" – it has little practical usefulness.

Sixth, our teaching should be appropriate for the emerging leaders we're building.

The average rural church planter in most countries probably does not need to study books of systematic theologies that are two inches thick. Of course, he does need some basic theological training but, realistically, in most cases, there are probably six or eight central facts he needs to know about each doctrine and those issues can be taught to him in a relatively short time. In the larger group or network of churches, there should be several leaders who are relatively expert in theology, but not every leader needs to be a theologian.

The following "Training Triangle" is a useful analogy:

- Many of us drive cars.
- Some of us can work on our own cars.
- A few of us are professional car mechanics.
- Even fewer work at dealerships.
- Fewer still work at car manufacturers.
- A small number of them are engineers.
- Even fewer are designers.

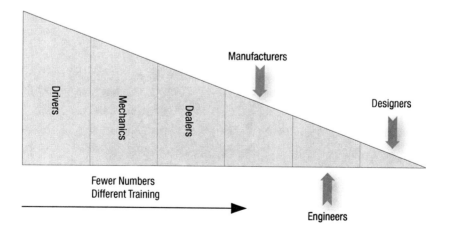

Each group needs a certain kind of training to be effective at what they do. It would be inappropriate to give a "driver" or "mechanic" the same type of training as an engineer or designer.

Applying the analogy to Christian leadership, there are many believers and a few workers. Some of those workers are teachers and a few teachers are authors and scholars. Consequently, they need varying kinds of training. Thus, it is inappropriate to expect a frontline church planter to have the same kind of training as an emerging Christian scholar. Our normal mode of training should not be of the "scholar" kind – that would be inappropriate and irrelevant.

Thus, "one size" will not "fit all." In Christian leader development we need varying kinds of training. It is not appropriate to expect every Christian leader to master the biblical languages and nuanced issues of church history and theological study.

Moreover, it is clear that while all engineers and designers will be drivers, not all drivers will be engineers, designers or mechanics. In the same way, the most effective Christian writers and scholars ("designers") will be those who can also *do* what they teach and write about.

Here are some of the questions that need to be asked to differentiate the particular training that is necessary at each level:

- What do they need to know?
- What do they need to do?
- What do they already know?
- What are they already doing?

The question naturally arises, "Who decides what kind of training particular emerging leaders need?" This is a question that must be answered, in the design process, by "action leaders" (those who are on the front lines of actual ministry, who will be more in touch with the practical realities of ministry), not only by "thought leaders" (the scholars and thinkers) (cf. 1 Cor. 3:10; Eph. 2:20). Paul, for example, was a brilliant thinker with a massive capacity for scholarship. Yet he was also a doer with extensive ministry capacity. And *he* was the one who wrote most of the epistles!

Finally, and most importantly, our teaching must be in the power of the Holy Spirit.

> *...all that Jesus began to do and to teach until the day he was taken up to heaven, after giving instructions through the Holy Spirit to the apostles he had chosen. (Acts 1:1-2)*

> *My message and my preaching were not with wise and persuasive words, but with a demonstration of the Spirit's power, so that your faith might not rest on men's wisdom, but on God's power. (1 Cor. 2:4-5)*

> *We have not received the spirit of the world but the Spirit who is from God, that we may understand what God has freely given us. This is what we speak, not in words taught us by human wisdom but in words taught by the Spirit, expressing spiritual truths in spiritual words. (1 Cor. 2:12-13)*

> *...our gospel came to you not simply with words, but also with power, with the Holy Spirit and with deep conviction. (1 Thess. 1:5)*

Jesus told us that apart from Him we can accomplish nothing of any value (John 15:4-5). How foolish we would be to trust merely in the effectiveness of our own human scholarship!

Thus, effective biblical instruction will be practical, relevant, appropriate and anointed by the Holy Spirit.

Individually or in your study group:

1. Please find biblical examples of the centrality of the Word of God in the training of emerging leaders.

2. Please find biblical examples of the practicality of the New Testament approach to the teaching of the Word of God.

Engagement Brings Change

There are two dimensions of leader competencies[39]:

1. Do you think?
   - Independent, *critical thinkers* go beyond manuals and procedures. They consider the impact of their own actions and the actions of others, and they are willing to be creative and innovative and to challenge the status quo when it is appropriate.
   - Dependent, *uncritical thinkers* do not consider possibilities beyond what they are told, and do not contribute to the creative nurturing of the organization. They accept others' ideas without thinking, and they stick to the traditional procedures – even when circumstances demand responsible deviation.

2. Do you act?
   - An *active* person demonstrates a sense of ownership. He participates fully in the organization, takes initiative in problem solving and decision making, interacts with coworkers at various levels, and goes beyond the bare necessities required by the job.
   - The *passive* individual needs constant supervision and encouragement by his supervisors. His level of involvement or interaction is limited to doing only what he is told to do. He avoids responsibilities beyond what the job specifically requires.

The effective leader is one who will both think and act. This is the kind of leader we must build.

---

[39] The following is adapted from *Healthy Followers: SpiritBuilt Leadership #11* by Malcolm Webber.

However, for the building process to be effective, emerging leaders must be engaged in it. They must be active learners. They cannot be passive recipients. They must be learners and not just listeners.

Traditional approaches to training treat people as if they were empty buckets – we just "fill them up" with learning and knowledge.[40] In reality, people are not buckets; they are more like muscles which need to be worked as well as fed.

Emerging leaders must be engaged:

- Spiritually – open, broken, and connecting with God.
- Relationally – accountable before the community, giving and receiving nurture and support.
- Experientially – actively doing ministry.
- Instructionally – through the various learning experiences.

Jesus designed a series of transformational learning experiences to build His disciples. For example, consider the incident of the feeding of the multitude:

> *When Jesus looked up and saw a great crowd coming toward him, he said to Philip, "Where shall we buy bread for these people to eat?" He asked this only to test him, for he already had in mind what he was going to do. (John 6:5-6; cf. Mark 6:37)*

Jesus designed a learning experience that intentionally engaged and challenged Philip.

Significantly, Peter's great revelation about Jesus being the Messiah came as

---

[40] One writer described it this way: Looking at most contemporary adult Christian formation curricula, we find teacher-centered models of transmitting information through lectures or presentations. When questions are asked of participants there is generally a "right" answer being sought and reflective dialogue is seldom designed into the lesson. Instead, Christian formation falls back on the "baby bird" pedagogy of students receiving from the teacher all that they need to learn.

the result of a question from His Teacher (Matt. 16:13-19). Frequently, Jesus asked questions – He didn't merely list the correct answers for everyone.

When we give people the answer prematurely they continue in the habit of just looking for quick answers; they don't grow in their own capacities to explore, discover and innovate. Thus, it's far better to ask, "What would you do?" or "How do you see this?" than to simply say, "Consider this…" and then proceed with giving the answer.

Jesus challenged and engaged His learners. Consequently, He knew His teaching was effective:

> …*Ask those who heard me. Surely they know what I said.* (John 18:20)

We must learn to do this too. Designing effective learning experiences is difficult but it is worth it. Of course, it is much easier to simply talk at people – we call this "teaching." However, people remember:

- 20% of what they hear.
- 40% of what they see.
- 80% of what they do.

Consequently, if you spend two hours preparing only to teach, you will achieve "20% success," whereas if you spend one hour preparing to teach and the second hour designing an effective learning experience that in some way engages the people in the learning process, you will potentially achieve much higher success.

Our goal is to build people; not simply to program "robots" so they do the right things the right way.[41] We need leaders who have developed the capacity to think and act. This requires engagement, not merely a filling

---

[41] Here is a useful distinction: We can "train" people to drive cars (they learn the basic competencies); we can "equip" people to solve problems (a deeper level of competencies so they can both think and act); we can "build" people to do well in every regard (dealing with all the 5Cs, not only competencies).

up with right knowledge.

The following table details some of the contrasts between "filling the bucket" and "engaging the learners."

Contrasts between "Filling the Bucket" and "Engaging the Learners"	
Filling the Bucket	**Engaging the Learners**
Monologue	Dialogue
Passive	Active
Teaching	Teaching and listening
Dry, boring	Stimulating
Emphasizes authority	Emphasizes effectiveness
Commitment to the curriculum	Commitment to the learner
Neat and tidy	Messy
Predictable	Unexpected/surprising
Individualistic	Community
Competitive	Collaborative
Exemplifies domination	Exemplifies humility
Plan driven	Need driven
Static	Flexible
Participants forget	Participants remember
Don't know how to use it	Can apply it
Kills potential	Develops potential
Dry source	A living spring
Cloning	Creativity
Program "robots"	Build unique people
Practically irrelevant	Relevant
Theory	Practice
Knowledge	Wisdom
Information	Transformation

Contrasts between "Filling the Bucket" and "Engaging the Learners"	
Filling the Bucket	**Engaging the Learners**
Presents answers	Problem-solving
Explain	Experiment
Gives answers	Asks questions
Hear	Do
What to think	How to think
A set program	Dynamic activity
Easy for the lecturer	Challenging for the teacher
Spectators	Participants
Participants' absence will be noted	Participants' absence will be missed
Minimal preparation by the lecturer	Life investment
Keep control	Empower – give away control
Produces "yes people"	Produces "think and act people"
Evaluate by tests	Evaluate by reflection, action, relationships, etc.
Short-term fruit	Long-term fruit
Acceptable results	Exceptional results
Much of it is never used	Every bit counts
Taking notes	Taking action
Explanation	Emulation
Stagnant	Growing
Potential	Actual
Knowing boats	Rowing boats

Listening is not necessarily learning; talking is not necessarily teaching.

Jesus was the Master Teacher, yet He didn't just talk all the time. In fact, a striking reality of the gospels is that, so often, Jesus' utterances were so brief.

Jesus designed learning experiences for His emerging leaders. Sometimes that involved listening to Him speak, but His strategy for leader development was not limited to that. Jesus used many methods and techniques in His teaching. For example:

1. Questions (e.g., Matt. 16:13-18; 22:41-46). This was one of Jesus' most common "teaching devices."

    A good question initiates a chain reaction of continuous learning.

2. Audio-visual aids.

    Jesus never used a PowerPoint or showed a movie. His creative budget was nothing. But He did use "audio-visual aids." He listened to His Father, and then simply made the best use of available objects, produced at the most strategic moment. Some examples:

    - Paying taxes: Matt. 22:15-22.
    - The simplicity, innocence and humility of children: Luke 9:46-48.
    - Faith, prayer, barrenness: Mark 11:12-14, 20-24.
    - Faith in the midst of the storm: Mark 4:35-41.
    - True giving: Mark 12:41-44.
    - True sight: John 9:1-7, 39-41.
    - Forgiveness: John 8:1-11.
    - Lazarus' resurrection: John 11:25.
    - Servanthood: John 13:4-17.
    - Jesus' own resurrection: John 20:27-29.

    As Jesus demonstrated, the effective use of a little can result in significant learning and change.

    Moreover, Jesus set His learning goals each time and then chose the aids, never the reverse order.

3. Correction.

Jesus corrected people in several ways.

Indirectly:

- He told a story to correct the proud: Luke 14:7-14.
- He spoke of the Gentiles and of His own example to correct pride and anger: Matt. 20:24-28.

Directly:

- He gave a warning to the over-confident Peter: Matt. 26:31-35.
- A simple look was enough to remind Peter of the earlier warning he had ignored: Luke 22:61-72.
- He gave a command to Peter: John 18:11.

4. Other teaching devices that Jesus used:

- His own example.
- Stories.
- Parables.
- Dialogues.
- Contrast: "You have heard that it was said… But I tell you…"
- Shock factor: Matt. 12:1-2; 15:26; Mark 3:2-5.
- Hyperbole: Matt. 5:29.

If lengthy explanations are, in fact, necessary, there are many ways by which we can get the information across without simply lecturing people:

- Homework.
- Handouts.
- Visuals.
- Break the content into questions.

Even secular educators know that "filling the bucket" is simply not the best way to build anyone, as the following extract from L. Dee Fink's study on college course design demonstrates[42]:

> ...most teachers seem to have difficulty figuring out what teaching activities they might use besides the two traditional standbys: lecturing and leading discussions. Studies have been done where someone goes into college classrooms and measures what teachers actually do. The number of times that a teacher even asks a question in a one-hour class period is remarkably low. In-depth, sustained discussions where students respond to other students as well as to the teacher are extremely rare. Although the language and vision of active learning have become a significant movement in North America, professional practice still lags woefully behind...
>
> What kinds of results does lecturing, even good lecturing, produce? A long history of research indicates lecturing has limited effectiveness in helping students:
>
> - Retain information after the course is over.
> - Develop an ability to transfer knowledge to novel situations.
> - Develop skill in thinking or problem solving.
> - Achieve affective outcomes, such as motivation for additional learning or a change in attitude.
>
> In a carefully designed test at Norwich University in England, teachers gave a lecture specifically designed to be effective. Students were given a test on their recall of facts, theory, and application of the content. They were allowed to use their own lecture notes and even a printed summary of the lecture. At the end of the lecture, the average level of the students' recall of information was 42 percent. One week later, even with the benefit of taking the same test a second time, students' recall had dropped 20 percent.

---

[42] The following is from *Creating Significant Learning Experiences* by L. Dee Fink (2003), pp. xi, 3-4.

In another study in the United States, students who took a year-long, two-semester course on introductory economics were compared with students who had never had the course at all. Over twelve hundred students in the two groups were given a test on the content of the course.

At the end of the course, students who took the course scored only 20 percent higher than students who had never had the course. Two years later, the difference was 15 percent. Seven years later, the difference was only 10 percent.

Collectively the results from these and other studies (many of which are summarized in an excellent study by Lion Gardiner, 1994[43]) suggest that our current instructional procedures are not working very well. Students are not learning even basic general knowledge, they are not developing higher-level cognitive skills, and they are not retaining their knowledge very well. In fact, there is no significant difference between students who take the courses and students who do not.

This is not to say that it is always bad to give a monologue. We know that Paul did this:

> *On the first day of the week we came together to break bread. Paul spoke to the people and, because he intended to leave the next day, kept on talking until midnight. There were many lamps in the upstairs room where we were meeting. Seated in a window was a young man named Eutychus, who was sinking into a deep sleep as Paul talked on and on. When he was sound asleep, he fell to the ground from the third story and was picked up dead. Paul went down, threw himself on the young man and put his arms around him. "Don't be alarmed,"* he said. *"He's alive!" Then he went upstairs again and broke bread and ate. After talking until daylight, he left. (Acts 20:7-11)*

---

[43] Gardiner, L. 1994. *Redesigning Higher Education: Producing Dramatic Gains in Student Learning.* ASHE-ERIC Higher Education Report 7. Washington, D.C.: George Washington University.

However, Paul was not merely giving course lectures to students behind desks; he was speaking spontaneously by the anointing of the Holy Spirit to the saints of God in someone's house.

> *My message and my preaching were not with wise and persuasive words, but with a demonstration of the Spirit's power, so that your faith might not rest on men's wisdom, but on God's power. (1 Cor. 2:4-5)*

> *This is what we speak, not in words taught us by human wisdom but in words taught by the Spirit, expressing spiritual truths in spiritual words. (1 Cor. 2:13)*

In addition, Paul did not speak for hours every day for years at a time to the saints at Troas. His ministry there was very brief.

Moreover, as we have seen from elsewhere in the Scriptures, we know that Paul did, in fact, use a variety of learning experiences in his leader development. He did not just lecture his emerging leaders.

Thus, it is not appropriate to use Paul's preaching in Acts 20 or elsewhere to justify endless monologues to students sitting in rows behind desks as the standard and central strategy for Christian leader development.

If we are going to build healthy Christian leaders we must become designers of effective learning experiences and not merely lecturers.

Individually or in your study group:

1. Please find biblical examples of emerging leaders being engaged in the process as they learned and grew.

2. Please examine your own processes of building people. Specifically, how can you raise the level of engagement?

Part 6

Effective Leader Development Will Be:

Intentional

精心设计，匠心独具

Elaborate design with rich creativity and originality

Responsibility

Leader development is not something you do "to" someone or "for" someone. A potter can only create the type of pot that the clay allows him to. Some clay is supple and elastic; some clay is crumbly and difficult to shape. The clay responds to the influences around it; it is not passive. It is the same with people. They are not simply the passive sum total of what we put into them. It is how they respond and interact with the various shaping influences around them that count.

> *Whoever corrects a mocker invites insult; whoever rebukes a wicked man incurs abuse. Do not rebuke a mocker or he will hate you; rebuke a wise man and he will love you. Instruct a wise man and he will be wiser still; teach a righteous man and he will add to his learning. (Prov. 9:7-9)*

Thus, responsibility for learning and growing resides in the emerging leader himself – as well as in the church community. Fundamentally, *building leaders involves providing opportunities for growth* – opportunities for learning, experience, responsibilities, relationships, resources, observing, suffering, etc. These opportunities will not magically produce the growth by themselves and there are no guarantees that specific individuals will take advantage of them.

When emerging leaders enter a development process, sometimes they have the attitude and expectation that change will be automatic. This is not true; in fact, sometimes they will be worse at the end, if they resist the demands of the process. Such a passive attitude is unhealthy and counterproductive. They must clearly be told that they will get as much out of the process as they put into it.

The following table details some of the contrasts between a holistic process and a traditional school.

Contrasts between a Traditional School and a Holistic Process	
Traditional School	**Holistic Process**
High dependency on teacher	Personal responsibility and initiative
Passive	Active
Get-it-done; goal oriented	A process; experience
Superficiality	Depth
Purpose: get a piece of paper (degree) at the end	Purpose: greater union with Christ and ministry effectiveness
Do as little as possible	Do as much as possible
Impersonal	Responsive
Irrelevant	Vital; life
Curriculum	Collage of relationships and experiences
Individualism	Community
Conformity	Reality
Head/intellect	Holistic/the whole person
Temporary	Permanent change
Informing	Transforming
Teaching	Learning
Us-them (adversarial relationship to teachers)	Us
Required/mandatory	Choice
Confusion	Unity of purpose
Hate learning	Love learning
Disengaged	Engaged/interactive
Competition	Teamwork/heartfelt cooperation
Scholarship	Relationship
Knowledge in	Knowledge in and out
Undisciplined	Disciplined
Boring	Creative
Humanistic	God-centered

Contrasts between a Traditional School and a Holistic Process	
Traditional School	**Holistic Process**
Isolation	Family
Self-sufficiency	Healthy dependency; reliance on the body of Christ
Alone	Community support
Low-commitment/cheap	100% commitment/cost is high
Subject is finished when the last paper for it is written.	Learning in all subjects continues for a lifetime.
Evaluation at the end to grade	Evaluation at the beginning, and all through, to inform design

To be effective, this process requires a high level of commitment and initiative on the part of the participant.

Sometimes we will know people who seem to have great leadership potential but they lack motivation. The following are some ways to help motivate people to learn and grow:

1. Pray for them. When faced with the lack of leaders in His own time, Jesus' response was:

   The harvest truly is great, but the laborers are few; therefore pray the Lord of the harvest to send out laborers into His harvest. (Luke 10:2)

   This is the key thing Jesus told us to do in the face of a leadership shortage: pray! However, this is often the last thing we actually do. The old adage, "When all else fails, pray" is utterly unbiblical. We should bring everything before God in prayer *before* trying anything else. The significance of Jesus' words cannot be overstated. His response when confronted with an acute lack of godly leadership was not to put on a "leadership seminar" but to pray.

174

Ultimately, it is God who works in emerging leaders "to will and to do according to His good purpose" (Phil. 2:13). So we should pray that God will raise up more leaders, better leaders, present leaders, future leaders. We should pray that God will move on the hearts of the ones in whom there is potential. God is the One around whom the issue actually revolves. Thus, prayer builds motivation.

2. Get their attention. Share with prospective leaders a vision of their potential in God. Share with them what they could accomplish, the lives and leaders they could transform, the cities and nations they could impact. Thus, vision builds motivation.

3. Teach them about the eternal rewards that a faithful leader will receive one day. Peter was addressing leaders when he wrote these words:

> *And when the Chief Shepherd appears, you will receive the crown of glory that will never fade away. (1 Pet. 5:4)*

Thus, reward builds motivation.

4. Give them assignments that create a desire to learn. Challenge them! The desire to learn is particularly high when new knowledge or skills are needed to do an existing job better or to complete an assignment that is altogether new. A person's latent desire to learn becomes a manifest *need* to learn when success depends on the mastery of new competencies. Thus, a specific need builds motivation.

5. Deal with them according to who they are – according to their giftings and passion – and not merely according to what the organization needs at the moment.

The more that people are focused on fulfilling their own specific destinies in God, the more motivated they will be to grow.

Everyone has certain "motivated abilities"; there are particular things that they are good at doing *and* want to do. The better we can match a person's given responsibilities (present and future) with his inward motivated abilities, the more willingly he will advance. Thus, gifting and calling build motivation.

6. Provide resources to assist them in learning. Such resources might include access to experienced people, training events, learning materials, etc. Thus, resources build motivation.

7. Encourage them constantly. When people start moving down a new path, they need frequent encouragement, especially when they encounter inevitable obstacles, unexpected problems and uncharted forks in the road. The unknown brings uncertainty and hesitation, so encouragement builds motivation.

8. Be careful to protect those who try and fail. Almost everyone admits that learning requires risk and inevitable mistakes, yet organizations are frequently characterized by zero tolerance for errors.

There is no more certain way for any leader to squash growth than to punish mistakes that are made in the spirit of learning. A learning environment must allow second chances, and present a tone that mistakes are acceptable as long as one learns from them. In fact, one should cultivate an atmosphere in which mistakes are expected! If someone makes no mistakes, that means he's not trying anything new, which means he's staying in his own comfort zone of what is already known and mastered, which in turn means he's not growing as a leader!

To grow, one must make mistakes. No baby ever learned to walk without falling down many times. No concert pianist ever learned to play the piano flawlessly at her first attempt. A teacher of ballet was once asked about her young ballerinas, "Could you ever tell when a young girl would become a *prima* ballerina?" The teacher responded that while all the girls were limber and very flexible when young, the future *prima* ballerinas were the ones who were willing to make fools of themselves. This is also the mark of a good leader: he is willing to take a risk and to try something new. Therefore, the builder must create an environment around the emerging leader that not only makes risk-taking possible, but also proactively encourages it.

The fear of failure paralyzes leadership. Imagine a wide and deep chasm between two cliffs with rocks at the bottom and someone is telling you to jump! This is an environment that does not allow mistakes. On the other hand, imagine a narrow and shallow chasm with a deep pool of cool, clear water at the bottom and someone is telling you to jump! This is an environment that does allow mistakes – especially on a hot day!

A friend taught one of my sons to walk on his hands. The first thing he did was to have my son stand up on his hands and then fall forward as he caught him. After doing this several times, my son overcame his natural fear of falling forward. The fear of falling forward is the greatest inhibitor to people learning to walk on their hands (in case you were wondering). But after my son actually fell forward a couple of times he realized that "failing" was not that painful after all. This emboldened him to continue to learn the new skill. Thus, to teach people to walk on their hands – or to do anything radically different – you must first provide an environment that reduces the cost of failure. It is this way with leadership. The builder must reduce the cost of failure for the emerging leader. He must make it possible for him to make a mistake without being crippled by it. In addition, he must overcome the tendency to rush in and rescue the person at the first sign of difficulty. Of course, if the person is about to expose himself or the community to unacceptable risk, then the leader must intervene; generally speaking, however, he must give the emerging leader some breathing room.

Thus, protection builds motivation.

While doing all we can to motivate the emerging leaders to learn and grow, at the same time, we must recognize that we cannot make someone become a leader against his own will. For example, Demas (2 Tim. 4:10) fell away after having ministered with Paul, the great apostle! Demas saw Paul's life, watched the miracles and heard his teachings, and he walked with God for a while, yet fell away. Moreover, Paul didn't blame himself for Demas' apostasy; it was Demas' own choice.

Judas Iscariot walked with Jesus Himself and yet fell away! In John 6:66-67, many of Jesus' disciples left Him and Jesus did not beg them to stay. It was their choice.

Thus, a person may have great potential, but he still must choose to respond to the opportunities offered him.

Leadership is hard. It comes with suffering, rejection and pain. There is often a high price to be paid if one is to lead. Consequently, not everyone – sometimes including people who are clearly called by God to be leaders – desires such responsibility. Many, unfortunately, hide their "talent" in the ground and never develop their potential (Matt. 25:25).

We should also recognize that someone may embrace the call to leadership later, in spite of their hesitancy now (Matt. 21:28-31).

Furthermore, we must recognize that sometimes we have plans for people's lives that do not necessarily reflect God's plans, and their rejection of us and our plans may not always involve a deeper rejection of God.

Individually or in your study group:

1. Please find biblical examples of leaders who did respond to the rigors of preparation for leadership.

2. Please find biblical examples of leaders who did not respond to the rigors of preparation for leadership.

Building Leaders Takes Time

There was once a young man who was exceptionally bright. When he was ready, his father went to enroll him in a fine university and said to the President of that school, "Since my son is so gifted, would it be possible for him to finish the courses in less than the normal time?" "It all depends on what you want your son to be," the wise president replied. "If you want him to be a great oak, it will take a while. But if you want him to be a cabbage, I can have him ready in no time."

Several months before Germany surrendered to the Allies, Franklin Roosevelt had expressed hopes that the Yalta conference would not last more than five or six days. Winston Churchill had a more realistic outlook: "I do not see any way of realizing our hopes about world organization in five or six days. Even the Almighty took seven."

We should not be unrealistic about the amount of transformation that is possible in a short period of time. No leadership learning process that is only brief can claim to produce a mature leader. It takes a lifetime to build a mature and seasoned leader.

For example, Moses spent years in the remote desert in preparation for his ministry. Joseph spent years in slavery and jail before he received his leadership assignment. Paul spent many years in preparation for his apostolic ministry.

Jesus only began to minister when He was thirty. Thus, Jesus spent 30 years of preparation for three years of ministry. Even more extreme was John the Baptist who spent 30 years in preparation for six months of ministry. That stands in contrast to our practices today – usually we spend a short period of time in preparation for a long period of ministry!

It takes time for a leader to become mature. Traditionally, learning institutions give their students degrees when they finish the prescribed course. Sometimes this can be quite damaging – both to the student and to his community – because the degree gives the *appearance* of a maturity and qualification that may or may not actually be present in the person's life.

There is a sarcastic Chinese idiom: "Pull the root up and help the plant grow faster." Of course, this does not work. In fact, it will probably kill the plant, even though in the short term the plant will appear to be taller.

In one Asian country, the influence of foreign ways of training has been quite negative. After a couple of years of training, young people graduate with degrees from schools that are funded and controlled by foreigners. These young people may not have planted a church in their lives, they have probably not spent time in prison for their faith, and some of them may not have even led anyone to the Lord. Yet, now they each have a degree – apparently, they're qualified. In contrast, the older leaders have planted hundreds of churches, won thousands of people to the Lord, have suffered for their faith for years in prison and have built the church movements with their own blood, sweat and tears – but, they don't have any degrees. Suddenly, who appears to be more "qualified" to lead? This dynamic has led to some degree of social disequilibrium within the church movements.

We must recognize that merely because someone has attended a training institution does not mean he is necessarily yet qualified to lead. It takes a long time to build a truly qualified leader. Our "fast-food" mentality will not succeed.

WHAT IS OUR GOAL?

Our goal in a short-term learning community, for example, should not be to build the whole "building" but to lay a good *foundation* for the person's life and ministry.

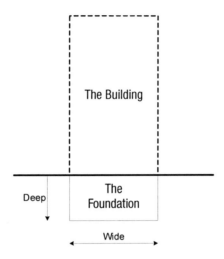

With a good foundation, a wonderful building can be built.

Thus, our goal should not be final and complete maturity, but the laying of a sound and comprehensive foundation in the life of the emerging leader.

Our goal should be *breadth of learning* as well as *depth of heart penetration*. We should not try to build *up* but to build *deep* and *wide*.

We should not attempt to produce mastery of every concept but rather broad exposure to a number of ideas and subjects.

Our purpose should be to teach the emerging leaders to pray, to get them connected to God in reality, and to impart passion of vision, zeal of heart, and a willingness to suffer.

We should also seek to teach them how to think, how to learn from their experiences and how to act. Moreover, we want to give them a love for learning. Our purpose should be to help the participant become a lifelong learner, one who will properly build on the foundation for the rest of his life.

Leader development occurs over a lifetime. Crash courses will not suffice. Extensive and diverse experiences can only occur over time, as does the learning that comes from experience. This is one reason why an individual's calling develops progressively over his or her lifetime – it rarely comes all at once.

Consequently, although you may be an important influence in another's life, you will rarely be the *only* influence. For example, there were multiple leaders involved in Paul's life as he grew: Gamaliel, Ananias, Barnabas, the other apostles, the leaders at Antioch, God Himself directly (2 Cor. 12:4). In Mark's life there were Jesus, Barnabas, Paul and Peter.

This is quite healthy. The best approach to mentoring involves bringing an emerging leader into as many quality relationships as possible. We tend to imitate both the good and bad elements of a mentor's life; this can be mitigated by having multiple mentors. In addition, each mentor will impact the emerging leader with his own unique style, strengths and priorities.

So, while a measure of protectiveness is appropriate, do not be possessive concerning the leaders you build. Instead, deliberately expose them to other men and women of God who can fill in the inevitable gaps. They don't belong to you but to God (1 Pet. 5:2-4).

Of course, it is easy to be possessive when you have invested so much time and energy in a person, but, if you really love him and believe in him, you will want him to be exposed to other influences and thus find greater strength and maturity.

In addition, the role of the learning community or formal training process should continue long after "graduation" with the facilitating of ongoing mentoring and coaching relationships, learning opportunities and challenging assignments for the maturing leaders.

In summary, we cannot seek a quick fix in the issue of leader development. It takes time to build leaders. We must have a long-term perspective similar to this ancient Chinese proverb:

If you are planting for a year, plant grain.
If you are planting for a decade, plant trees.
If you are planting for a century, plant people.

Individually or in your study group:

1. Please find biblical examples of leaders who spent a long time in preparation for their ministries.

2. Please find biblical examples of the personal involvement of *several* leaders in the life of an emerging leader.

People Are Different

People are different; leaders are different. This reality should be reflected in a healthy development process in two ways.

1. People grow and learn at different rates, in different ways, from different things. Therefore, an effective process will use a variety of learning experiences to assist participants' transformation.

    There is a need for caution as we address this area. There is no doubt that everyone brings a different set of interests, abilities, personality factors, developmental levels, social and cultural experiences, and emotions to bear on learning opportunities. But it is an error to say that these constitute distinct "learning styles."

    Some people have made claims about learning styles that go far beyond any supporting evidence. One common claim asserts a difference between so-called "left-brained" and "right-brained" individuals. In reality, both hemispheres work cooperatively in all people who have a healthy brain. Others divide people into distinct groups, such as "verbal learners," "visual-spatial learners," etc. This artificial division is not supported by the research, and it suggests that people learn only in one way, consistent with their supposed learning styles. It also erroneously suggests that the way we learn is fixed and unchanging.

    It is a fact, however, that particular teaching material can usually be taught in a variety of ways. In addition, the available research suggests that everyone learns better when the content is approached in more than one way – both visual and verbal, as well as through hands-on active learning. Thus, a healthy teaching model will use a variety of learning experiences to augment the lecture-only method that has been used almost exclusively in traditional schools.

A collage of different kinds of learning experiences will provide more effective learning for everyone.

2. People's callings are different (1 Cor. 12; John 21:22); therefore, our learning goals for them should reflect these differences.

So, for example:

- While there should be a core content track that everyone completes, not everyone will need to go as deeply into certain areas as others might, depending on their individual callings.
- Ministry projects need to be individualized.
- Appropriate mentors and coaches should be given to emerging leaders in their particular areas of calling.

PRACTICAL IMPLICATIONS FOR BUILDERS

In view of the above, effective leader development will be individualistic (with consistent core principles). Each person is a unique tapestry of callings, strengths and weaknesses, and his developmental needs must be matched with developmental opportunities and approaches (and be consistent with the ministry needs of the community as well).

This has several important implications. It means that leaders who build leaders must first know them. They must step beyond superficial acquaintance and the temptation to resort to routine "methods" of development. It is not sufficient for the mentoring leader to give the emerging leader "the book that we use for leadership training" and have him read it, and then ask him the prescribed questions. The mentoring leader, after taking the time to get to know the new leader in a variety of situations, must design a multi-faceted strategy of development that will be most appropriate for him. Over time, this strategy will need to be corrected and adjusted, perhaps completely reworked. This whole process will take considerably more time and effort than the usual "here's the book or course we always use" method, but will yield far superior results.

As we have mentioned before, this, in turn, means that one leader can build only a few other leaders – if he will do it properly.

Individually or in your study group:

1. Please find examples in the Scriptures where a leader varied the learning experiences that he gave his disciples.

2. Please find examples of leaders who were very different in their callings and experienced very different development processes.

Both Team and Individual Learning Contexts Must Be Provided

The most effective leader has learned to integrate the disciplines required for working in teams with the disciplines of individual initiative. Therefore, an effective development process will balance individual and team contexts.

Two extremes are common today: those who think that everything must happen in a team context, and those who think that everything must happen in an individual context. We need both.

Leadership has multiple responsibilities in both contexts – so our processes of development should too.

To work effectively in teams, requires growth in:

- Accountability
- Encouragement
- Patience
- Death to self
- Vulnerability
- Community
- Relationships
- Communication
- Endurance
- Preferring others before oneself
- Balancing compliance with assertion
- Appropriate compromise
- Flexibility
- Appreciation for different perspectives
- Challenging one's own mindset
- Listening
- Dealing with conflict

- Humility
- Confronting
- People skills
- Scheduling

To work effectively individually, requires growth in:

- Discipline
- Self-control
- Clear vision
- Honesty
- Determination
- Finishing what one starts
- Realistic self-knowledge
- Focus
- Dependency on God
- Organization
- Self-management
- Motivation
- Goal-setting
- Initiative
- Responsibility
- Integrity
- Sacrifice
- Being strong in many areas

Just as each of the different machines in the fitness center work different muscles, so our leader development processes must develop the various aspects of the leader's life and ministry.

TEAM-BASED LEARNING

By causing the emerging leaders to take responsibility for their own and their peers' learning, a team-based approach can dramatically enhance the quality of learning for the emerging leader – in almost any subject.[44]

There are three ways in which small groups can be used in learning:

Casual Use of Small Groups	Cooperative Learning	Team-Based Learning
· "Turn to the person next to you and discuss this." · Relatively spontaneous exercises, with no advance planning. · Not much attention paid to group composition or learning strategy. · Adds variety and a degree of active learning.	· Intentional and frequent use of small groups. · Inserting group activities into an existing course, without changing the overall design. · Group activities are planned and carefully structured. · Attention is given to group formation, participants' roles, accountability, etc. · Generates more sophisticated learning and thinking capacities than casual use.	· Makes small group work the primary activity of the participants in the particular course. · The "small groups" become cohesive "learning teams." · Often requires a change in the structure of the course. · Participants learn the content and how to use it, they learn about themselves and each other, and they learn how to interact with others on major tasks.

As the following graphic shows, if team-based learning is done well, participant learning is greatly improved in quality.

---

[44] Much of the following is adapted from *Team-Based Learning* (2004), edited by Michaelsen, Bauman Knight and Fink.

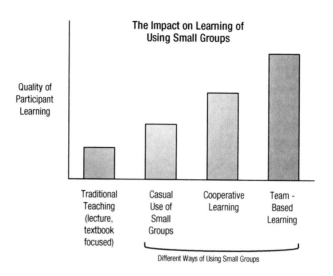

The Impact on Learning of
Using Small Groups

Quality of
Participant
Learning

| Traditional Teaching (lecture, textbook focused) | Casual Use of Small Groups | Cooperative Learning | Team - Based Learning |

Different Ways of Using Small Groups

In fact, studies have shown that 98 percent of teams will outperform their own best member on learning-related tasks!

WORKING GROUPS AND TEAMS

Working groups and teams both consist of two or more people who interact in a common activity. What distinguishes teams from working groups is that teams are characterized by:

- A high level of individual commitment to the welfare of the whole group.
- A high level of trust among group members.

For a group of people to become a "team" requires:

- Time interacting together.
- Access to resources.
- A challenging assignment that becomes a shared goal.
- Frequent feedback on individual and group performance as well as relationships.

When this happens, teams become capable of:

- Inspiring a high level of individual effort.
- A willingness to challenge each other without fear of giving offense because of a high tolerance for open and honest communication.
- Working together effectively; relational cohesion.
- Successfully accomplishing complex and challenging assignments.

HEALTHY TEAM-BASED DYNAMICS

The following are some recommendations regarding team-based learning:

- The participants themselves should be responsible for defining and distributing roles, rather than having their roles simply assigned to them. The participants need to learn how to build and function within a team. In addition, they are in the best position to recognize multiple and different kinds of contributions from individual team members: some participants will generate creative ideas for the team to consider, others will be stronger in analyzing and assessing those ideas, others will be good at managing the group work, while others will be the team spokespersons.
- If possible, team size should be five to seven participants. This size (more than four) will put significant resources and perspectives at the team's disposal, while avoiding a size that makes it too hard for all members to participate (more than eight).
- It is important that leaders spend time with the team participants, helping them both to understand and to improve group dynamics. This interaction is best accomplished throughout the learning process (as opposed to only an initial general teaching on teams).
- Team assignments should promote both learning and team

development. This two-fold goal of team-based learning must be kept in mind.

- Teams should be carefully formed, by the leader and not the participants, keeping the following in mind:

    - Sometimes two participants who do not work together well should not be on the same team. Other times, this might be appropriate.
    - Teams should be as evenly matched as possible, with regard to participant capacities.
    - Teams should be as diverse as possible. This diversity will initially appear to be counterproductive,[45] but after a while will become a clear asset, since it brings a rich resource base to the team.
    - Teams should not be changed too quickly. It takes a while (typically 20-25 hours or more of interaction) for participants to get to know each other, to trust one another, and to figure out how to get something done well together.

- Participants must be held accountable. In traditional school settings, the students are not usually accountable to anyone other than the teacher. Team-based learning, however, offers meaningful opportunities for peer-accountability – the participants evaluating one another's contributions to the team – in both work performance and relational issues.
- Team assignments should not be able to be easily divided up (e.g., writing a long paper in sections that can be split up), but should require interaction (e.g., complex decision-making).

DESIGNING TEAM-BASED LEARNING EXPERIENCES

Team-based learning is an entire strategy, not merely an incidental teaching technique. It is a series of learning experiences in a designed

---

[45] While diverse teams usually will initially be less effective than homogeneous ones, in the long-term they will be more effective.

sequence, not just an individual activity that is plugged in wherever convenient.

The following graphic presents a simple approach to designing team-based learning experiences.

Within the overall plan, there are three phases: preparation, application and assessment.

- In the preparation phase, each group does some initial reflection or exploration about the subject. This gets them thinking and orients them to the content matter. Second, participants do reading assignments to learn the basic concepts or there is teaching (or a combination of cohort teaching and individual reading). The goal, at this point, is not for them to gain an in-depth mastery or full comprehension of everything, but to get a good introduction to the information and ideas on the subject. Then they come together for an evaluation to ensure that they have sufficient grasp of the material to proceed to the application phase (e.g., a multiple choice exam could be completed both individually and then in the team). Then the participants can verbally respond to the evaluation. After this, the leaders and teachers will have a good idea of what areas need to be strengthened. Then some teaching can follow, focusing only on the areas that participants were not able to grasp already. This preparation phase will result in a moderate level of understanding of the material.
- In the application phase, alternating between individual and team work, the participants put the content into practice by together answering questions, solving problems, creating explanations, or doing some kind of ministry. To be effective, this practice should be accompanied by immediate feedback.
- After they have practiced applying the content for an appropriate time, they are ready for the assessment phase. After some final review, the leader will watch them do the ministry, or, in the classroom, the teacher will grade them on a paper or exam.

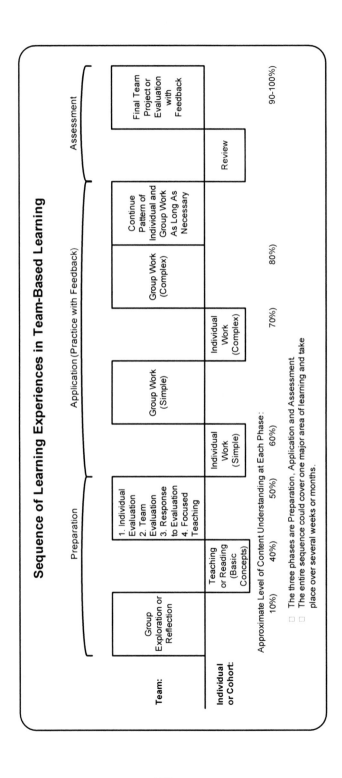

Sequence of Learning Experiences in Team-Based Learning

	Preparation			Application (Practice with Feedback)			Assessment	

Team:

| Group Exploration or Reflection | Teaching or Reading (Basic Concepts) | 1. Individual Evaluation 2. Team Evaluation 3. Response to Evaluation 4. Focused Teaching | | Group Work (Simple) | | Group Work (Complex) | Continue Pattern of Individual and Group Work As Long As Necessary | Final Team Project or Evaluation with Feedback |

Individual or Cohort:

| | | | Individual Work (Simple) | | Individual Work (Complex) | | Review | |

Approximate Level of Content Understanding at Each Phase:

10%   40%   50%   60%   70%   80%   90-100%)

☐ The three phases are Preparation, Application and Assessment
☐ The entire sequence could cover one major area of learning and take place over several weeks or months.

197

This should also include self-assessment, peer assessment and community-assessment.

This progression from simple to complex can be seen in how Jesus built leaders. He began with teaching and modeling for His disciples. Then He quickly gave them some relatively simple ministry responsibilities (e.g., John 4:2), which grew in complexity (e.g., Matt. 10:1-16), as He continued to work with them, until finally He gave them the Great Commission!

A PRACTICAL EXAMPLE

This first example is for training emerging leaders in evangelism.

Preparation: first, the emerging leaders reflect, in their teams, about their previous experiences related to evangelism and/or their biblical understanding of the purpose and nature of evangelism. Perhaps they might also interview experienced evangelists about their experiences. Second, the leader shares some teaching on evangelism in written or spoken form, setting forth the need for and nature of evangelism, along with some appropriate strategies and methods. Then the emerging leaders are evaluated to ensure they have learned the basics, followed by some follow-up teaching in weak areas. Then application begins.

Simple Individual Work: the emerging leaders each prepare short presentations of the gospel along with their own testimonies.

Simple Team Work: they give these presentations in front of their own teams, who respond with feedback. After receiving this feedback, each one gives the same presentation again, with improvements being discussed.

More Complex Work: individually, they create strategies for sharing the gospel in the local neighborhood. Then, in their teams, with the help of experienced mentors, they evaluate each other's strategies and forge a single strategy that they will then implement. As a team they now go and do it!

Ongoing Work: depending on the situation, the work can increase in complexity to the point of planting a new church in the area or even reaching the lost in another people group.

A THEOLOGICAL EXAMPLE

This second example is for teaching doctrine.

Preparation: first, the emerging leaders, in their teams, reflect on the particular doctrine by asking or answering biblical questions related to it. Second, the teacher shares some core biblical teaching on the doctrine in written or spoken form. Then the emerging leaders are evaluated to ensure they have learned the basics, followed by some follow-up teaching in weak areas. Then application begins.

Simple Individual Work: the emerging leaders are given a series of Scriptures on which to reflect. Individually, they are to classify and interpret the passages in some defined way according to the core points of doctrine they have learned.

Simple Team Work: as a team, they take their individual work and prepare one final report. These reports are shared between teams, with each team expected to give at least three points of improvement to each written report.

More Complex Work: individually, each is given details of one historical error regarding the doctrine with the assignment of preparing a biblical response. Then, in their teams, they debate with each other, with each team member, in turn, taking the position of speaking for or against the error. After this debate, the team prepares a final written report on the error and its biblical response. These reports are shared between teams, with each team expected to give at least three points of improvement to each written report.

Review and Evaluation: now the teacher reviews what they have covered, followed by a final evaluation.

THE FRUITS OF TEAM-BASED LEARNING

Team-based learning that is effectively designed and executed will result in:

- Greater understanding of the content.
- Capacity to apply the content to ministry situations, problem-solving, decision-making, etc.
- Well-developed relational skills for working effectively with others.
- Individuals valuing the team approach to ministry.
- Increased desire and capacity for life-long learning.
- The teachers are freed from the burden of having to "cover all the material" since it is the participants who do much of this work themselves.

Individually or in your study group:

1. Please find biblical examples of leaders functioning effectively in a team context.

2. Please find biblical examples of leaders functioning effectively in an individual context.

Effective Leader Development Is a Complex, Experiential Collage

Even though we can identify certain of its elements, leader development is not a simple and orderly step-by-step procedure of moving through a series of predictable and successive points. In reality, leader development is a rather chaotic, complex and multifaceted experiential *collage*.[46] It is an experiential collage of diverse people, relationships, influences, assignments, tasks, responsibilities, duties, deadlines, opportunities, pressures, crises, blessings, sufferings, rejections, successes, mistakes, etc., that all work together to build the emerging leader.

Thus, an effective leader development process is not a neat series of courses but a fiery immersion in real-life, real-time experiences, reflecting the complicated and fundamentally difficult nature of Christian leadership, bringing deep heart issues to the surface to be dealt with, and compelling the participant to look utterly to God for everything in his life and ministry.

The following table details some of the contrasts between a leader development "collage" and a traditional curriculum.

Contrasts between a Traditional Curriculum and a Leader Development "Collage"	
Traditional Curriculum	**Collage**
Teacher oriented	Learner oriented
Time-bound	Flexible
Sequential	Dynamic

---

[46] In India, we call this a "masala." A masala is a wonderful mixture of many spices.

Contrasts between a Traditional Curriculum and a Leader Development "Collage"	
Traditional Curriculum	**Collage**
Classroom	Field-based
Teaching lectures	Teaching, mentoring, coaching, etc.
Textbooks	Experiential
Predetermined	Continually redefined
Safe	Volatile

INTENTIONAL DESIGN

Throughout the Scriptures we see the importance of design to God:

> *See that you make them according to the pattern shown you on the mountain. (Ex. 25:40; cf. Solomon's Temple, Ezekiel's Temple)*

> *...you are God's building. (1 Cor. 3:9, NKJV)*

Jesus was intentional in building His leaders. He created a transformational collage (spiritual, relational, experiential and instructional) around His emerging leaders. It was not haphazard; He built them according to design. We also must learn to create effective designs – transformational collages – for leader development.

> *By the grace God has given me, I laid a foundation as an expert builder, and someone else is building on it. But each one should be careful how he builds. (1 Cor. 3:10)*

FOUR KINDS OF LEADER DEVELOPMENT STRATEGIES

There are four specific ways that the ConneXions model, as detailed in this book, can be implemented:

First, *foundational learning communities for emerging leaders* are local church-integrated learning environments that focus on holistic leader formation, that integrate the spiritual, relational, experiential and instructional dynamics of transformation, and that are intentionally designed to accomplish this goal. "Foundational" learning communities are for emerging leaders. Typically, each one will involve 10-20 participants for a one-year period, alternating time spent in the learning community with time spent in the field with experienced mentors. The goal is to lay a strong foundation for the emerging leaders' lives and ministries.

Second, *ongoing learning communities for existing leaders* are small teams of existing leaders who meet regularly for training that is intentionally integrated into their lives and ministries. These teams may last for one or more years. They also focus on holistic leader formation, integrate all four dynamics of transformation, and are intentionally designed to accomplish this goal. "Ongoing" learning communities are for existing leaders who are already engaged in ministry work. The goal is more advanced development of the leaders' lives and ministries.

Third, *short-term trainings* are several day (or several hour), needs-driven events for those already in positions of leadership who cannot leave their ongoing ministry obligations for extended periods of training. Each event might include a large number of leaders.

Finally, the leaders' incorporation of ConneXions principles in their day-to-day *"lifestyle leader development" of the emerging and existing leaders* in their ministries will bring very powerful and pervasive transformation to their churches and ministries. "Lifestyle leader development" refers to the intentional incorporating of ConneXions principles by leaders in their unofficial, unscheduled, impromptu training of others as well as their deliberate mentoring and coaching relationships. A great deal of learning in a leader's life (perhaps 80%) occurs informally and the quality of this learning can be significantly improved when those involved understand the ConneXions principles and intentionally apply them as they build others in the normal course of daily life and ministry, as well as during "official" learning times.

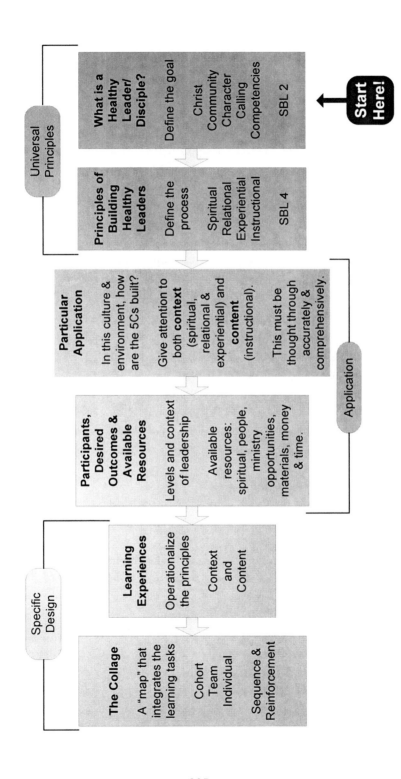

Universal Principles

What is a Healthy Leader/Disciple?

Define the goal

Christ
Community
Character
Calling
Competencies

SBL 2

Principles of Building Healthy Leaders

Define the process

Spiritual
Relational
Experiential
Instructional

SBL 4

Particular Application

In this culture & environment, how are the 5Cs built?

Give attention to both **context** (spiritual, relational & experiential) and **content** (instructional).

This must be thought through accurately & comprehensively.

Application

Participants, Desired Outcomes & Available Resources

Levels and context of leadership

Available resources: spiritual, people, ministry opportunities, materials, money & time.

Specific Design

Learning Experiences

Operationalize the principles

Context
and
Content

The Collage

A "map" that integrates the learning tasks

Cohort
Team
Individual

Sequence & Reinforcement

Start Here!

A PRACTICAL MODEL FOR DESIGNING A PROCESS

The following is a simple method by which a process for building leaders in any culture or context can be designed.

This same process can be used to design a half-day training or a one year learning community – or anything in-between.

The method is summarized in this graphic:

Step One: Starting at the right, we begin by defining what a healthy leader is. If we do not have a clear understanding of our goal, the process of development will be hard to define.

Please see *Healthy Leaders: SpiritBuilt Leadership #2* by Malcolm Webber for a complete discussion of the 5C model of healthy leadership. This is our goal: an effective, healthy Christian leader is a man or woman who knows God in a daily experiential relationship, was formed and lives in supporting and accountable community, has a strong character, knows the purpose of God and is able to present it with credibility, clarity and passion, and has the necessary gifts, skills and knowledge to lead the people in the accomplishment of this purpose – and is continually growing in all five areas.

"The key to design is to clearly define." First, we must clearly define our goal. Then, we must define the process that will achieve that goal.

Step Two: Having defined what a healthy leader is, we then need to establish biblical principles of how such a leader is formed. This current book is our attempt at doing this.

Steps One and Two are universal in nature. They are foundational biblical principles that will work in any culture or context. The exact form that they will take will vary considerably from place to place and time to time, but the principles are universal.

Now we move to application of the general biblical principles. This is how the appropriate form for each context will be created.

Step Three: This step begins to define how the universal biblical principles are operationalized in any given context. This is accomplished by asking the question, "How is each of the 5Cs built in our context in a way consistent with the universal principles of leader development?" For the final design to be effective, this step must not be rushed. It must be thought through accurately and comprehensively.

Traditionally, in leader development design we have focused mostly on instruction. However, we must give significant attention to all four of the "dynamics of transformation": spiritual, relational, experiential and instructional. This is how lives are changed! When all four dynamics are strongly present in a design, spiritual life is nurtured, relational capacities are strengthened, character is developed, calling is clarified and deep leadership capacities are built.

The author has asked thousands of Christian leaders around the world, from a wide variety of cultural backgrounds, these questions, "How were you built? What were the influences that formed and molded you as a leader? What made you the leader you are today?" Almost invariably, the answers include such things as parents, role models, examples, mentors, sufferings, responsibilities, rejections, failures, challenging assignments, etc. It is rare that someone will mention a course, and when they do, it is often the teacher who personally impacted their lives and not so much the content that they remember.

This should not surprise us, since an honest study of the gospels will reveal that Jesus did exactly this with His disciples. His strategy was not merely instructional; He also created a transformational context of leader development, including spiritual, relational and experiential elements.

This was also the practice of the early church:

They devoted themselves to the apostles' teaching and to the fellowship, to the breaking of bread and to prayer. (Acts 2:42)

All four dynamics were present:

- The apostles' teaching – instructional.
- Fellowship – relational.
- The breaking of bread – experiential.
- Prayer – spiritual.

To say that we need all four is not to devalue content. We must have strong content; indeed, instruction is one of the four key dynamics of transformation of this model of healthy leader development. However, by itself, content is not sufficient. To build *lives* we must design transformational contexts that are strong spiritually, relationally and experientially.

To illustrate this, consider the following example. Suppose we want to build evangelists. We could begin with an *experiential* component by simply sending them out to share the gospel with unbelievers. "Just go and do it!" Will that work? Will they learn anything about evangelism? Certainly they will!

Now let's include a *relational* dimension by sending them out with experienced evangelists who they can watch and who will watch them, and encourage and correct them. Clearly this will work even better.

Now let's add a strong *spiritual* element by having our emerging evangelists join with intercessors before going out. They will pray and cry for the lost, entering into God's burden for those without Christ. Then, when they go out to evangelize they are also to look to God for help, asking Him who to go to, and waiting upon Him inwardly for the right words to speak. This will work better still!

Finally, let's give them some *instruction* – a good course on the meaning and nature of evangelism, studying God's plan of salvation, a simple way to share the Gospel and one's own testimony, some common objections to the Gospel and how to respond, etc. Now we're building strong evangelists!

This simple example demonstrates the power of designing learning experiences that give strong attention to all four dynamics of transformation. This is how lives are changed; this is how leaders are built!

Just as we must intentionally build all of the 5Cs of healthy leadership (Christ, Community, Character, Calling and Competencies) so we must design processes of leader development that include all four dynamics of transformation (Spiritual, Relational, Experiential and Instructional). None can be neglected!

On the following page, there is a chart that lists examples of activities that fall under each of the four dynamics.

Dynamics of Transformation

Spiritual

- Praying
- Being prayed for
- Prayer walking
- Meditation in the Word
- Memorization of Scriptures
- Receiving healing and deliverance
- Forgiveness
- Listening to one's conscience
- Move of the Holy Spirit
- Power encounters
- Visions, dreams, prophecies
- Worship
- Praise
- Waiting on God/Listening
- Devotions
- Reflection
- Contemplation
- Journaling
- Fasting
- Giving
- Silence
- Solitude
- Spiritual rest
- Retreats
- Music

Experiential

- Challenging assignments
- Learning by doing
- Success
- Fruitfulness
- Suffering
- Responsibilities
- Failure
- Ministering
- Receiving ministry
- Praying for others' healing and deliverance
- Exercising gifts
- Career/work/job
- Field Trips
- Travel
- Cross cultural experiences
- Sickness/health
- Evangelism/sharing Gospel and own testimony
- Relief work/social service
- Pressure
- Deadlines
- Persecution

Relational	Instructional
· Friends	· Teaching
· Family	· Questions
· Spiritual mothers and fathers	· Dialogue
· Examples	· Facilitation
· Role models	· Round table discussion
· Mentors	· Discussion groups
· Coaches	· Reading
· Teams/working groups/small groups	· Problem-based learning
· Networking	· Audio/visual, PowerPoint
· Reflection together	· Simulations
· Prayer for each other	· Interaction with leader/teacher
· Communion and Love Feast	· Internet
· Foot-washing	· Role play
· Support	· Brainstorming/whiteboarding
· Nurture	· Quizzes
· Biographies and testimonies	· Call out
· Informal instruction	· Puzzles/riddles
· Encouragement	· Creative media, poetry, songs, drama
· Accountability	· Q & A
· Evaluation	· Panel
· Communication	· Debate
· Counsel	· Interviewing
· Correction	· Sharing notes
· Enemies	· Learning projects
· Conflict	· Homework
· Rejection	· Bible studies
· Reconciliation	· Demonstrations
· Serving/serving together	· Speeches
· Fun/recreational activities together/sports	· Show and tell
· Fellowship	· Stories and analogies, metaphors, parables
· Eating together	· Case studies
· Hospitality	· Storytelling
· Visitation	· Kinesthetic activities
· Care	· Consultations/workshops/ seminars

This third step of design might yield ideas such as the following:[47]

Christ is built in an emerging leader's life through:

- Ensuring the person is genuinely saved.
- Personal relationships with people who know Christ.
- Daily systematic meditation on Scriptures that reveal God (such as John 13-17).
- Times of individual and group prayer, worship and fasting.
- Prayer with him for the filling of the Holy Spirit.
- Prayer with him for Christ to be formed in his life.
- Prayer with him for deep repentance and deliverance from spiritual oppression.
- Practical teaching on fellowship with God. The Word of God reveals Jesus.
- Having teachers who know God and reveal and impart passion for Him.
- The teaching of the cross with personal reflection on its practical meaning for daily life.
- Studying the psalms and learning different ways to pray.
- Studying historical revivals.
- Studying true and false spirituality.
- The use of devotional materials.
- Short devotional stories and testimonies of sacrifice and abandonment to God.
- Exposure to the life stories of people who have walked with God, as they share the realities of their own spiritual lives.
- Reading and reflecting on biographies of men and women who knew God, especially from cultures and backgrounds similar to the emerging leader.
- Regular meetings with an intercessor with whom the emerging leader will share his heart and from whom he will receive intense and ongoing prayer.
- Regular meetings with a pastoral coach to whom the emerging

---

[47] The following lists were generated by a group of Asian church network leaders.

leader will be accountable and transparent concerning his life and struggles.

- Being required and assisted by the community to resolve the problems of life, dealing with offences, bitterness and unforgiveness which are obstacles to relationship with God.
- Watching his life and his reaction to circumstances, especially bad ones.
- The emerging leader sharing his personal testimony of Christ's reality in his life (Philemon 6).

Community is built in an emerging leader's life through:

- Teaching and meditation on the triune nature of God as the foundation for all human community.
- Biblical study on the nature of the church, characteristics of church life, generational issues, pastoral care, etc.
- Shared experiences.
- Existing leaders making themselves available to build relationships with the emerging leader.
- Being required and assisted by the surrounding church community to work through relational issues with others.
- Acts of service.
- Practicing giving and receiving affirmation.
- Experiences in which the emerging leader shares his deep personal experiences with those he trusts.
- Prayer and worship with others.
- Doing team assignments.
- Ministering with others.
- Traveling together.
- Living together at times.
- Practical experiences to give emerging leaders the opportunity to learn how to get along with each other.
- Formal and systematic accountability to others such as a pastoral coach.
- Study and reflection on personality and culture.
- Study and reflection on male and female roles.

- Doing some fun activities with others.
- Visiting people in their homes.
- Biblical teaching and reflection regarding family relationships: husband-wife, parents, children.
- Watching the leaders and teachers themselves engage in practical church life.
- Opportunities to build relational skills.
- Submission to appropriate accountability and correction in the church.
- Daily prayer for the community, helping to bear its burdens.
- Practical teaching on basic manners.

Character is built in an emerging leader's life through:

- Godly people living before the emerging leader so their lives and characters impact him. The leaders and teachers must do what they teach. They must be honest and transparent, with the courage to confront their own personal errors and flaws, being willing to change. Ministry examples must be chosen for their character as well as their competencies.
- Teaching on character, with biblical and historical examples.
- Teaching about relationships with other churches and ministry ethics.
- Accountability required of the emerging leader in relational and practical ways.
- The study of suffering and its place in the leader's life – biblically and historically.
- Discipline. Appropriate rules should be put in place and maintained with correction being given as necessary.
- The emerging leader being corrected for his errors and affirmed and encouraged for his successes. Affirmation brings zeal for what is right.
- Study of servant and abusive leadership.
- Study of the fruit of the spirit with personal reflection, honest self-evaluation and application.
- Teaching on financial health and accountability.

- Dialogue with experienced leaders concerning ethical dilemmas they have faced – both personal and ministerial.
- Receiving challenges from different circumstances and environments for the growth of endurance, patience, etc.
- Intentional assignments for different emerging leaders according to their individual character needs; e.g., submission, patience, humility.
- Paying attention to events and circumstances, making use of every opportunity to teach and learn character.
- Testimonies from living examples of godly character – either through their stories or in person.
- Submitting to serving tasks.
- Introducing appropriate pressure to give the emerging leader the opportunity for self-knowledge and growth.
- Exposure to accounts of leaders who have endured great sufferings for their faith.
- Community assessment of the emerging leader's character, revealing "blind-spots," as well as self-assessment.

Calling is clarified in an emerging leader's life through:

- Vision being revealed through interaction with leaders and teachers and through interaction with God in prayer and worship.
- Opportunities to practice different ministry callings to see if they are a "fit."
- Practical ministry assignments accomplished with an experienced ministry mentor.
- Teaching on how to know God's will.
- Various learning exercises – teaching and personal and group reflection – on purpose, life vision, spiritual gifts, motivated abilities.
- Emerging leaders sharing with each other their own experiences and passions, as well as their most appreciated models and examples in life and ministry.
- Personal times with experienced leaders for explanation, clari-

fication, encouragement, prayer and mutual support.

- Being encouraged when he goes through difficult times as he ministers according to his calling.
- The use of assessment tools to clarify calling.

Competencies are built in an emerging leader's life through:

- Relationships with experienced leaders.
- Learning and doing.
- Effective interactive teaching.
- Study of beneficial materials.
- Learning experiences related to knowledge of biblical studies, basic doctrines, biblical interpretation, church history, etc.
- Learning experiences related to practical ministry capacities such as listening, communication, time management, dealing with conflict, leading change, creativity, strategic planning, management skills, relational skills, cross-cultural ministry, church planting, etc.
- Challenging ministry assignments.
- The development of thinking capacities.
- Studying and memorizing Proverbs, learning wisdom.

Please note that the above lists are not by any means exhaustive.

Step Four: In the second part of the application process, we must closely consider the following:

- Our intended participants. Who are they? Urban or rural? Socio-economic status? Level of education? Spiritual experience?
- The desired outcomes. What do we hope our participants will become? What is their level and context of future leadership? Will they be the top leaders of national movements, local church leaders, etc.?

- Our available resources:
  - What people do we have who can interact with the partici-
    pants as pastors, coaches, spiritual mothers and fathers,
    ministry mentors, intercessors, role models, teachers,
    etc.?
  - What practical ministry opportunities are we able to
    provide for the emerging leaders as they grow?
  - What study materials are available in the target language
    and culture – books, videos, tapes, etc.?
  - How much money is available for this training? Who
    will pay for it? If outside money is involved, what will
    its long-term effects be? What is the plan for long-term
    financial sustainability?
  - What is our time frame? Will this be a full-time one month
    training process, one day a week for two years, full-time
    for one year, etc.?

Step Five: Now we begin to build the specific design by creating learning
experiences that operationalize everything we've defined to this point.
These learning experiences should be:

- Diverse. This will create a varied and creative environment for
  change. All four dynamics of transformation must be incor-
  porated.
- Intentional. Each learning experience should intentionally
  focus on one or more of the 5Cs. This will provide balance for
  the whole process.
- Experiential. Certainly some of them could have a strong
  academic component, but we should avoid the mind-numbing
  traditional ruts.

The Four I/A model helps us to design effective learning experiences.

The Four I's/A's
Inductive or Anchor
· Relate what you're about to teach to previous experience. People learn best by connecting the new to the old. Connect the learners with what they know and their own unique context. This will usually be more effective with older leaders since they have more life experience. · Relate what you're about to teach to existing biblical knowledge. Show where it fits and why it's important. This will work well for both emerging and existing leaders.
Input or Add
· The content. The new instruction. Invite the learner to examine new input.
Implement or Apply
· Do something with the new content, implementing it. · Apply it practically. · Analyze it biblically. · The teacher should also share some application from his own life and ministry.
Integrate or Away
· Move new learning into life practice. · This may be a projection task that invites emerging leaders to imagine integrating the new learning in their ministry or life. · Or it may be a task that happens later, after the learning time, with some element of reporting or feedback.

Step Six: Now we build the collage itself, creating a "map" that defines how we will move through the learning experiences, how they all fit together in a cohesive manner building on each other effectively. This collage will incorporate the various contexts of individual learning experiences as well as team and cohort (the entire group of emerging leaders who are engaged in the process together) ones.

At this point, both sequence and reinforcement must be addressed.

- Sequence is the intentional ordering of learning experiences. We should begin with simple, clear and relatively easy learning experiences before advancing to more complex ones. Thus the learning experiences should be arranged so that each new one builds on the last and prepares the emerging leaders for the next. It is often necessary to break complex ideas or issues into several steps within a learning experience or by using several learning experiences, moving from the simpler to the more complex. If the sequence is not appropriate for the emerging leaders, they will become confused and/or show resistance. In addition, we should alternate between individual and team experiences.

  This progression from simple to complex can be seen in Jesus' leader development. He began with teaching and modeling for His disciples. Then He quickly gave them some relatively simple ministry responsibilities (e.g., John 4:2), which grew in complexity (e.g., Matt. 10:1-16), as He continued to work with them, until finally He gave them the Great Commission!

- Reinforcement refers to the deliberate repetition of information, attitudes and skills. This repetition should be diverse, engaging and interesting. The need for it will vary considerably from person to person and thus requires personalized attention.

DESIGN TEAMS

It is a good practice to establish a design team. This team should have the following characteristics:

- Not too big a group.
- People who can think strategically and conceptually.
- People who are practically-oriented and knowledgeable about

the realities of the ministry environment.

- People who have significant hands-on leadership experience, have been successful in ministry and have experience in training.
- Learners who are willing to experiment and explore.
- People who are willing to commit to designing new forms of indigenous leader development.
- People who are able to get together on a regular basis and work on this.

Ideally, the design team will be a strong partnership between teachers (who bring the science) and leaders (who bring the art). The result will be leader development that is disciplined and alive!

This design team can then:

- Pray and brainstorm ideas.
- Collect resources.
- Design learning experiences and effective collages of leader development.

As they do this frequently, they will become very good designers of intentional leader development.

Of course, at all times, our plan is subject to His!

It is hard to build leaders well. It is a truly complex task. It is so complicated, in fact, that only God can do it; and with God's help, we will succeed! To the new leaders at Philippi, Paul wrote: "being confident of this, that He who began a good work in you will carry it on to completion until the day of Christ Jesus" (Phil. 1:6). This is our strong confidence: God will do it!

Individually or in your study group:

1. Please find biblical examples of the complexity of leadership –
    in both testaments.

2. Please find biblical examples of each of the four dynamics of
    transformation and their role in leader development.

New Leaders for the Churches!

Michael Paige is the senior leader of a small group of churches in a largely unreached city. God is moving wonderfully in this city and many people are coming to Christ. But there are not enough trained leaders to shepherd the new believers. Michael knows he must train new leaders.

He contacts a seminary in another city and asks them for help. They respond very graciously, offering to send two of their full-time teachers each week.

For the next twelve months, every Saturday, these two teachers come and spend six hours giving lectures to Michael's chosen group of thirty emerging leaders. Each night during the week, after work, the young leaders study the books their visiting teachers have left for them and complete their written assignments. They study Old and New Testament Survey, Systematic Theology, Biblical Ethics, Apologetics and Church History.

After one year, the graduation is held and the president of the seminary gives the address and congratulates the new graduates on their good grades before handing them their diplomas. Michael is deeply relieved that now he has some qualified leaders.

Two days after the graduation, Michael meets with his new leaders and asks them, "How will you now work with the new believers and the existing churches? And how will we continue to reach out to the lost in our city? What will you do?"

Silence falls as the new leaders look blankly at each other. Michael wonders what the problem is.

Individually or in your study group, read the parable of a Christian leader. Analyze the situation and offer suggestions for improvement. Use what you know about the 5Cs, the four dynamics of transformation, the 18 Principles, and the need to design for both context and content to help you shape your suggestions.

Try using these four questions to help you analyze the story. Your suggestions for improvement will come from Question 4.

1. What is happening here – good and bad? (Observation)

2. Why is it happening? (Interpretation)

3. What problems does it cause? (Application)

4. How can this be improved? (Change)

A Letter from an Emerging Leader

I am an emerging leader. You are an existing leader. I'm so grateful that God has placed you in my life. I really need you!

First, please teach me the Word of God – because the Truth is life. The Truth can change my thinking. It can transform my life. But I need you to teach me with the anointing and conviction of the Holy Spirit; not only with words, but with conviction and power.

However, please don't simply teach me; I need you to share your life with me. Don't teach me only theoretical ideas; be transparent with your life. Tell me about your experiences of God, about the victories you have seen, and about the failures you have had. Your hopes, your disappointments, your joys, your frustrations – share it all with me.

In addition to instructing me, please genuinely engage with me in my life. I need to know that you really care about me, that your intention is not merely to train me to do certain things and then send me out as a foot-soldier in your army. Please don't use me. I need to know that you love me and are committed to me. Express this commitment to me in variety of ways. When I do things well, affirm me. When I make errors, hold me accountable; with love and gentleness, correct me.

Please give me responsibilities; responsibilities that are appropriate to my maturity. Some should be mundane tasks to build servanthood in my life. But also give me important things that increase my vision and help clarify my calling. Carefully design these responsibilities so they stretch me and force me to learn, to grow, and to look to God for success.

As I fulfill those responsibilities, don't leave me alone; be with me and encourage me. And not only you; please build other relationships around my life. Encourage other mature brothers and sisters in the church to embrace me as their spiritual son. Help them know how to engage with me in practical and meaningful ways in my life. In their lives I'll see what it means to be a mature believer. I'll see it. Not only will you teach me about it; I'm also going to see it. I've got to see it!

I need to see marriages that, while not perfect, are healthy. In a little while I'm going to be married. I need to know what it means and how it works. You taught me that the husband should love his wife as Christ loves His church. Because of the Presence of the Spirit upon your teaching, I was moved and touched by it; I was so moved I wept when I saw this in the Scriptures. But I still need to see it in life. I must see it. I've got to see it in lives around me.

I need those people also to walk with me in life. As I'm going through experiences, responsibilities and pressures, I must know that I'm not doing it by myself, but there are others who are with me, committed to me, affirming me, encouraging me, and praying for me. In their lives I will see how to endure. I know I need to endure; you taught me this well. But I need to see it. I need to be with you when you go through some terrible fiery sufferings. I'll watch you endure. That's how I'm going to remember. That's how I will really get it.

So please take me with you sometimes. Let me watch you as you do leadership stuff. I love your teaching, but I need to see you actually do it!

As I walk with you and as we do things together, I will learn more deeply what it means to be a leader. I will watch you as you make difficult decisions in hard situations. I will watch you as you pray for the people you are serving, and when you weep for them. I will be with you when you are patient with people. I will be with you when you correct those who are wrong. That's how I will learn to do it myself.

As you look at my life, help me see the purpose of God for me and give me assignments. Continually look for opportunities to put me to work. Never allow me to be passive. Don't let me sit at a distance and be quiet.

Draw me out saying, "Hey, come on my son! Look at the vision of God. Look at what God's doing, and what you can be and do in Him. Come on!" Affirm the calling I've got on my life. Affirm that God has given me a wonderful purpose. Always be in front of me, saying, "Come on! You can do it!" When I respond, "No I can't," tell me, "Yes, you can." Affirm me. Challenge me. Then send me off to go and do it, with others around me.

Please intentionally connect me with others around me – with ministry partners and teams. Wisely connect me with other people who complement how God made me. Sometimes you should intentionally connect me with people with whom you know I will have conflicts. And we'll start to get into little disagreements, and some sparks will fly. And then I'll feel bad. I'll notice that you have been watching me during these conflicts, and I'll feel as if I have let you down. But then I will see that you are not upset. You will reach out to me with care and love. You'll say, "Hey, come on! Let's dig into this. There are some bad things in your life, aren't there? And this relationship, this circumstance, has brought up the worst. So, let's dig it out now."

In the past, I was afraid to let anyone touch those deep inner things, but you've built a strong relationship. I know you are for me, I know you are committed to me. So, cautiously, I will open up a little bit. And you'll pray with me and look over some of the pains in my life. We'll face it together. Gently you'll encourage me to forgive those who have wronged me. You'll lead me through the releasing of bitterness and pain. You'll help me understand this conflict that I had in the relationship – that the relationship didn't cause the issues in my heart; it simply gave them an opportunity to be exposed. As you work with me through this, I will understand more how God deals with me in the struggles of life. He allows me to go through the fire. I'll remember that you taught me about this from Peter's first letter; now I know it in my life. Other spiritual mothers and fathers will gently nurture this transparency and honesty in my life.

In dealing with all this, submitting myself to Truth, submitting myself to God, through these deep, nurturing, caring, accountable relationships, in the midst of the challenges, complexities and pressures of life, God will change me. I'll find myself freer. I'll realize that I'm learning the true nature of the Christian life. I'm learning what the nature of leadership is. Not just the doctrine. Not just some "eight points" that someone says is important. But I'm really getting it. I'm seeing it. I'm being changed. I'm being changed by the Truth of the Word, in the power of the Spirit, in the midst of a loving, nurturing, accountable family, going through the deep, challenging experiences of life. I'm finding God.

I'll see Him in your life, and in the lives of the others who are around me, committed to me. I'll learn how to pray, because I watch you pray. I'll watch you worship God. In this way I'll learn what it means to worship God. I'll see in the Word the wonderful revelation of how I'm made just to worship Him. I will understand this. And then I'll do it, because you will encourage me to do it. I'll know how to do it because I have seen you do it. As I do it, I'll be changed even more by the Spirit. I'll come to know Him. I'll learn how to turn my heart to Him, to find Him, to see Him, to know Him. I'll know God. And I'll have good doctrine about God too.

I'll learn what it means to be a friend because I have friends. They will love me and remain committed to me even when I act ugly. They will always be there for me. They won't reject me. You will be there for me. Then I'll start to realize what you've been teaching me, that God says He will never reject me. What you taught me about Hosea will start to make sense to me – that even though Hosea's wife was not faithful, he remained faithful to her. And God said to His people, "That's how I treat you. I will never abandon you." I will remember when you taught me – at that time my heart rejoiced, and again there was such a beautiful presence of God that I wept in the teaching. But now I'll see it more clearly, more richly, because I see you do it. I understood the Scripture, but I wasn't sure what it looked like in life. How would it work? I had many questions. But now you have answered my questions, not just in your teaching but in your life. Because I see it, now I know. I thought I knew it, and in a way I did. But now I really know it. It has changed me.

In all the difficult times, I will not be alone; you will be there with me. I know that I only need to give you a call. If I come over and knock on your door, you'll be there for me. And not only when I come after you, but you will come after me too, and hold me accountable. Even at times when I want to run, when I want to hide, you won't let me. Not in a dominating way, but with affirmation, you will reach out to me. You'll say, "Come on! Let's face the issues, let's face this stuff together. You can rise above it. Together let's cry out to God. In the midst of the difficulty and pressure, together let's look to God, to see His hand in your life."

I will learn what it means to work with people, by watching you. I'll learn how to work with nice people. I'll learn how to work with difficult people. I'll learn what it means to have a healthy marriage, because you will intentionally invite me to see what really happens in marriages. And when I think I have found my wife, you will help us. You will also connect us with mature couples, and they will share their lives and struggles transparently with us.

I'll find that all the junk and worldliness that used to be in my life will drop off. I'll be changed by the Truth. I'll be changed by the work of the Spirit. I'll be changed in this loving community around me, as we walk together in the experiences, sufferings and challenges of life. God will build true holiness in my life, making me a man of integrity – not merely someone who knows the right things to say, not merely someone who knows how to act properly when others are watching, but a man of true integrity – because you have worked deeply with my life. You were not content with superficial things. You created experiences for me that gave me the opportunities to show what was really in my heart. Then when all that was there came out, you were there for me, helping me to understand it according to the Truth of the Word of God, helping me to submit to Him, to give it to the Lord, and genuinely receive His grace – not just know about His grace, but actually receive it. Something changed in me; inwardly, in my heart, genuine integrity was born. I know I'm not perfect. I know I'm not going to be perfect, because when I look at you I don't see perfection. So I know it's going to be no different for me. But I know I'm going to do well, because I have seen it in your life.

I want to be like you. As I see the way that you seek God for your purpose and the destiny of the church, as I watch you do that, my heart will be gripped, because I see your heart gripped. I'll see your passion, your vision. As I see the sacrifice of your life – as I see that – that will bring forth my willingness to sacrifice. As I see your passion for the lost, reflecting Jesus' heart, my heart will be changed.

I'll watch as you look at all the complicated things around you, all of the complexity of what's happening in your life and ministry. I'll see you are not overwhelmed. But you respond to this complexity with brokenness and a deeper looking at the Face of God. I'll see you do that. I'll be watching you. I will see how you are able to look at all that complicated murky stuff and then make a decision and say, "Here is where we are going to go." By the leading of the Spirit, you establish a clear direction. That will affect me. I'll remember that for the rest of my life. I will learn how to do the same thing myself, without even realizing that I'm learning this. I will find myself in complicated situations and my first response will be to look to God – because that's what you did. I've seen you do it many times. So without even thinking about it, I will do the same thing. Somehow your abilities to think strategically and make decisions will have rubbed off on me. I'll have developed this capacity to think. Not only to think, but also to act. I'll have seen you do it. I'll have watched you so many times where a lesser man or woman would have been paralyzed with indecision. But you took the responsibility. You didn't take the easy way out. You took the responsibility in spite of the complexity and, at times, the cost. I'll have seen you do that numerous times. I didn't realize that as I was watching you, somehow it affected me too. Now I'll do the same thing, because through your teaching you have changed me. By bringing me to God again and again in so many different ways, you have changed me. By your example and your interaction, you have changed me, as you walked with me through the difficulties and challenges of my life.

Then I will notice that you've given me opportunities where I can serve others in the same way – where I can be to them what you have been to me.

One day, suddenly, I will realize that people are looking to me for leadership. And I will recognize that God has been raising me up to lead and serve His people. Through other lives around me, through His Presence, by His Word, in the experiences of life, God has changed me, prepared me, built me. I know I'll never be perfect, but now I can do it. I can lead. I've been built – well built.

Conclusion

For the last 20-30 years, there has been a great deal of focus around the world on evangelism and church planting. This has borne much fruit. Every day, tens of thousands of people come to Christ. Every week, several thousand new churches are planted. There has been remarkable church growth in many parts of the world.

However, there has not been corresponding attention given to leader development during this time. Consequently, today we have a deficit of Christian leaders in the existing churches, with new churches being planted all the time. It is an increasing deficit.

There are now more than 2.2 million evangelical churches worldwide. 85% of these churches are pastored by men and women without training. But, even if all training institutions would operate at 120% of capacity, they could train less than 10% of this number.[48]

In addition to this crisis of *quantity* of new leaders, we also face a crisis of *quality* of existing leaders. Clearly, our traditional methods of leader development simply have not delivered either the quantity or quality of leaders that today's churches need.

Why must we keep doing things the same way, when we know it doesn't work very well?

Of course, we don't have to!

As we face the great challenge of leader development in the thriving church of the 21st century, we must dare to question our traditional methods. Are they really biblical?

---

[48] Source: TOPIC *Ministry Update*, Sept. – Dec. 2009.

To borrow and reconceptualize a phrase, we need to "de-school" the way we build Christian leaders.

We need to move from a teaching-centered (or information-centered) paradigm to a transformation-centered paradigm. This involves change in three areas:

1. **The goal.** We need to move:
   - *from* focusing on academics *to* building the whole person,
   - *from* grades *to* capacities,
   - *from* degrees *to* maturity,
   - *from* outputs (graduates) *to* outcomes (changed lives and effective ministry capacities).

2. **The process.** We need to move:
   - *from* the factory *to* the family,
   - *from* a list of courses *to* a collage of learning experiences in a relational web,
   - *from* telling *to* learning,
   - *from* "understand and remember" *to* "think and act,"
   - *from* monologue *to* dialogue,
   - *from* covering content *to* testing ideas,
   - *from* classroom instruction by appropriately-degreed and full-time teachers, *to* personal in-the-field interaction with experienced and full-time ministry leaders.

3. **The design.** We need to move:
   - *from* starting at the beginning with what we need the course to cover, *to* starting at the end with what the leader needs to become,
   - *from* teaching courses *to* designing learning experiences and relational contexts,
   - *from* crowding courses together ("pasted pieces") *to* cohesive integration ("shaped wholes"),
   - *from* marketing franchises *to* working with national leaders to create truly indigenous designs for leader development.

We need to move *from* blaming leaders for their failure, *to* taking responsibility for inadequate leader development processes that set them up for failure in the first place.

Today, many Christian educational institutions have embraced a new goal. They have recognized the deep need to build character, spiritual life and practical ministry capacities. However, they have not gone to the second step. *A new goal requires a new process.* An academic process is entirely appropriate for an academic goal, but a holistic goal demands a holistic process. The new wine needs a new wineskin!

As we noted in the Introduction, Jesus' method of building leaders was a holistic process:

> *He appointed twelve – designating them apostles – that they might be with him and that he might send them out to preach and to have authority to drive out demons. (Mark 3:14-15)*

He created a *transformational context* around His emerging leaders:

1. A *spiritual* environment, involving relationship with God (with Himself as well as with the Father through prayer).
2. A *relational* web, involving relationship with a mature leader (Himself), and relationships with others (the community of the disciples).
3. An *experiential* context, involving challenging assignments, pressure and a diversity of learning opportunities.

Then, in that context, He instructed them – the *content* of development.

If we will do it His way, if we will give as much attention to the spiritual, relational and experiential context as we have traditionally given to the instructional content, we will have much better success!

And the harvest will not be wasted.

Books in the *SpiritBuilt Leadership* Series
by Malcolm Webber, Ph.D.

1. *Leadership.* Deals with the nature of leadership, servant leadership, and other basic leadership issues.
2. *Healthy Leaders.* Presents a simple but effective model of what constitutes a healthy Christian leader.
3. *Leading.* A study of the practices of exemplary leaders.
4. *Building Leaders.* Leaders build leaders! However, leader development is highly complex and very little understood. This book examines core principles of leader development.
5. *Leaders & Managers.* Deals with the distinctions between leaders and managers. Contains extensive worksheets.
6. *Abusive Leadership.* A must read for all Christian leaders. Reveals the true natures and sources of abusive leadership and servant leadership.
7. *Understanding Change.* Leading change is one of the most difficult leadership responsibilities. It is also one of the most important. This book is an excellent primer that will help you understand resistance to change, the change process and how to help people through change.
8. *Building Teams.* What teams are and how they best work.
9. *Understanding Organizations.* A primer on organizational structure.
10. *Women in Leadership.* A biblical study concerning this very controversial issue.
11. *Healthy Followers.* The popular conception that "everything depends on leaders" is not entirely correct. Without thoughtful and active followers, the greatest of leaders will fail. This book studies the characteristics of healthy followers and is also a great resource for team building.
12. *Listening.* Listening is one of the most important of all leadership skills. This book studies how we can be better listeners and better leaders.

Strategic Press
www.StrategicPress.org

Strategic Press is a division of Strategic Global Assistance, Inc.
www.sgai.org

2601 Benham Avenue
Elkhart, IN 46517
U.S.A.

+1-574-295-4357
Toll-free: 888-258-7447